WARTIME SUMMER

True Stories of Love,
Life and Loss on the British Home Front

CAROLINE TAGGART

WARTIME SUMMER

JOHN BLAKE

Published by John Blake Publishing,
The Plaza,
535 Kings Road,
Chelsea Harbour,
London SW10 0SZ

www.facebook.com/johnblakebooks ❶
twitter.com/jblakebooks ⬛

First published in paperback in 2019

Paperback ISBN: 978 1 78946 124 4
Ebook ISBN: 978 1 78946 130 5

British Library Cataloguing-in-Publication Data:

A catalogue record for this book is available from the British Library.

Design by www.envydesign.co.uk

Printed and bound in Great Britain by Clays Ltd, Elcograf S.p.A.

1 3 5 7 9 10 8 6 4 2

John Blake Publishing is an imprint of Bonnier Books UK
www.bonnierbooks.co.uk

For all those people – of my parents' generation –
who lived through the Second World War and shared
their memories with me.
Without them, my generation would not be
where we are today.

CONTENTS

INTRODUCTION

'It was the best of times, it was the worst of times...' Charles Dickens wrote those words about the French Revolution in *A Tale of Two Cities*; for some of the people I spoke to in the course of researching this book they could equally well apply to living through the Second World War. Many who are now in their eighties – children during what their generation still calls 'the war', as if there had been none since – recall happy times and little hardship. They didn't miss bananas, oranges and ice cream because they had never known a world in which these foods featured. Yes, sweets were rationed, but when you got them, they were a treat. You were thrilled to be given a bicycle for your birthday and you looked after it not just because you loved it but because you knew that if anything happened to it, you wouldn't be getting another one.

Even those in the cities considered nightly bombing raids

as a fact of life at worst, a great excitement at best; more than one of my interviewees recalled thinking that a new baby sister was more of a nuisance than anything Hitler could throw at them. Those who are a little older – teenagers and young adults during the war – acknowledge the horrors but still refer to a time when everyone was in the same boat, hardships were shared and endured, and families and communities supported each other. 'If we were going to die, we would die together,' they say. 'We just got on with it.'

Another thing few people missed was a holiday. It seems incredible now, when so many can jet off to the Caribbean at the drop of a hat, but until the late 1930s the average worker in Britain was not entitled to paid leave. The Holidays with Pay Act of 1938 granted certain employees (not all) one week's paid holiday a year. Northern industrial towns had a long-standing tradition of 'Wakes Week', when the factory or mill was closed for its annual maintenance and everyone went on holiday at once, with each town choosing a different week so that Blackpool and Bridlington weren't inundated; but through the year the workers would have contributed to a Wakes Saving Fund or 'Going-Off' Club into order to pay for it.

Small wonder, then, that most people didn't take holidays, or just managed a few days at the seaside. They simply couldn't afford anything else. Only the very well-to-do or those who needed them for work had cars, so the vast majority of travel was by train. When war broke out and the slogan 'Is Your Journey Really Necessary?' discouraged civilians from occupying space on overcrowded trains that was needed for service people and freight, staying at home and making your own entertainment was, for many, the only option. The comfortably-off did better, but even they were hampered by petrol restrictions and the fact that beaches were covered with barbed wire as a defence against invasion.

Amusing yourself at home had its compensations, though. One feature of wartime summers that those who were children remember most clearly is the blissfully long evenings provided by double summer time. In spring 1940, the clocks went forward as usual, but they didn't go back in the autumn; in spring 1941, they went forward again, meaning they were two hours ahead of Greenwich Mean Time. This was a government policy designed to make it easier for people working long hours to get home in the blackout and also, it hoped, to save fuel. Of course, it made for darker mornings, with the same complaints that 'daylight saving' provokes today, but for the children it meant playing outside in the traffic-free street until way past their normal bedtime. One of the people I interviewed quoted a poem – 'Bed in Summer' – that turned out to be by Robert Louis Stevenson:

> In winter I get up at night
> And dress by yellow candle-light.
> In summer, quite the other way,
> I have to go to bed by day…

> And does it not seem hard to you,
> When all the sky is clear and blue,
> And I should like so much to play,
> To have to go to bed by day?

Although it must have been written fifty years earlier, he felt it was very apt for what was happening to children during the war years.

Summer, for the purposes of this book, embraces much more than the holidays people didn't have. Several of World War Two's major events took place in what can loosely be considered the summer: war was declared in early September 1939 and declared over (in Europe at least) in May 1945, so including those two months provides a tidy framework. The evacuation of Dunkirk and the D-Day Landings, in the Junes of 1940 and 1944 respectively, were both closely followed by retaliatory bombing campaigns, which made those summers less than idyllic for those involved. Against a background of these crisis points in the war, more generic, less time-specific stories unfold: stories of evacuation, rationing and entertainment – such as it was.

Much of what follows is the result of interviews I conducted with friends and relations, or with the friends and relations of friends and relations. Some is gleaned from diaries and letters written at the time. All these people had very different experiences, from the evacuees who had four different homes in six years to the children whose happy-go-lucky childhood was carefully cocooned by protective parents; from the East Enders who played in bombsites to the achingly young officers who had to deal with the horrors of Dunkirk and D-Day. Many of the people I interviewed said apologetically, 'I haven't told you very much' and I would try to explain: 'It's a jigsaw puzzle. You give me three pieces, someone else gives me three pieces, sooner or later I have the thousand or so that

I need.' The interesting thing was that this particular jigsaw didn't come in a box with a picture on it. It is assembled in a way that I couldn't have predicted when I began work on it, to show courage, humour, humanity in the face of fear, sorrow and cruelty – in, perhaps, the best and worst of times.

CHAPTER 1

'YOU'VE GOT TO COME IN. THERE'S A WAR ON'

Throughout the summer of 1939, it was clear that war was coming. Long before it was finally declared in September of that year, all but the most blindly optimistic knew that it was inevitable. Adolf Hitler had been Chancellor of Germany since 1933, and during those six years his National Socialist (Nazi) Party had been crushing political opponents and beginning the persecution of the Jews that would lead to over 300,000 fleeing the country and six million dying in what came to be known as the Holocaust.

Hitler also rearmed Germany in violation of the terms of the Treaty of Versailles, which had been imposed at the end of the First World War. He set about re-establishing his country as a major European power, invading neighbouring territories with a view to creating a larger home state for ethnic Germans.

On 30 September 1938, a European conference in Munich agreed to Hitler's annexation of the Sudetenland (a largely German-speaking part of modern Czechia). British Prime Minister Neville Chamberlain returned waving that famous piece of paper and declaring that it represented 'peace for our time'.

It didn't.

Hitler invaded Poland on 1 September 1939. Britain and France issued an ultimatum for him to withdraw; it was ignored and, on a sunny Sunday morning two days later, Chamberlain spoke on BBC Radio, announcing that 'this country is now at war with Germany'. Describing this as a 'bitter blow', he declared that Hitler's actions showed that he could only be stopped by force and concluded his address with these words:

> Now may God bless you all. May He defend the right. It is the evil things that we shall be fighting against – brute force, bad faith, injustice, oppression and persecution – and against them I am certain that the right will prevail.

For most of his listeners, it was a melancholy, if not entirely unexpected, end to the summer holidays.

*

As early as 1935, with the threat of war already looming large, the Home Office had formed the Air Raid Precautions Department – the ARP – to supervise civil defence measures. Hundreds of thousands of people joined as volunteers. Local wardens were to be responsible for, among other things, ensuring that the blackout was respected, reporting bombings, sounding sirens and escorting members of the public to shelters.

Herbert, living in Luton, joined in 1937. He wrote scathingly of the details of form-filling that being a member of the ARP entailed, as well as learning to deal with various types of gas mask and fabricating accidents so that volunteers could practise first aid. Then came the night when he was instructed to don a uniform and go out into the town to recruit more volunteers:

I was told to array myself in a suit of proofed protective clothing, supposed to make one immune from the bodily irritations of harmful liquid likely to be used in warfare. This had obviously been designed for a man seven feet tall and with a sixty-inch chest. However, after much improvisation, I found myself arrayed in a waterproof jacket the size of a bell tent, plus-fours of like material and a pair of rubber boots, knee-high, one size seven and one size eleven. The whole ensemble being completed by the wearing of a tin hat of small size, but of a weight that increased the load on my mind.

So clad, I presented myself for public approval. The effect was appalling. Mothers drew their small children into the protective custody of abbreviated skirts as I passed by. Horses shied, and strong men blanched. Then while I dispensed pamphlets to all and sundry, the total effect of twelve men so garbed was stunning. It must have been, for we secured volunteers.

The element of farce persisted, even when war broke out and a first siren went off. It turned out to be a false alarm:

> We studied and learned from our mistakes and during the months that followed put the lessons into effect. My darts, solo [whist] and dominoes improved out of all knowledge. I could answer the phone without being nervous and for the first time in years I spent the nights away from my family. The time following the commencement of hostilities was an anticlimax. For twelve months, Auxiliary Fire Service men polished brass, painted white lines and played solo. First-aid parties did stretch drill, tied reef knots and played solo. Wardens inspected gas masks, went through gas chambers and played solo.

Even so, Herbert and his colleagues knew that the real thing couldn't be far away. In the meantime, the British government found other ways of spreading information as war approached. Jean, living in Portsmouth, recalls:

> Everyone smoked in those days and each packet of cigarettes had a card in it, with a picture on one side and a bit of information on the other – there was a series about footballers, another about flowers, all sorts of things. People used to collect them and stick them in an album, which you bought for a penny from the shop where you bought your cigarettes. In the summer of 1939, when everyone knew war was coming, they issued

war ones, telling you about the war and precautions and what you should do.

The album in which you stuck those particular cigarette cards, produced by W.D. & H.O. Wills in association with the ARP, proclaimed them as being of National Importance. It also featured a foreword by Sir Samuel Hoare, Home Secretary, immediately before the war, assuring the public that…

> Air Raid Precautions are not mysterious. They are based on commonsense suggestions and the things recommended cost very little and demand ingenuity and improvisation rather than expenditure. Even some of the more elaborate recommendations can be carried out quite easily in cooperation with a neighbour.

The cards themselves illustrated, among other things, how to protect the walls and windows of your home against bomb blast by stacking sandbags outside them; how to equip a 'refuge room' in your home; and how to put out an incendiary bomb with water from a hose pipe. It was a pragmatic, 'make do and mend' approach which, along with the idea that everyone was in this together, would become all too familiar in the years that followed.

For many, the summer of 1938, culminating in the Munich Conference in September, marked the beginning of the end of normality. John, aged nine, recalls the moment he became aware of the threat:

I remember going with my aunt and a friend of hers to the flower show in Southport. I think it must have been in September 1938, because I associate it with Munich. There was an announcement over the Tannoy that any reservists should report for duty on the following Monday. That shook me – I remember asking what a reservist was.

Shortly afterwards, he entered boarding school in Wakefield:

In the spring and summer terms which followed – the first half of 1939 – German teenage boys appeared in school on Saturdays with some regularity, stayed perhaps a fortnight and then disappeared. We'd often have an outing on Saturday afternoons – a coach trip to Harewood House or something like that – and when we came back to school for tea, there they would be. It was only a trickle, perhaps two or three at a time, but it happened quite often. The school was evidently on one of the escape routes from Germany and it was there that the boys awaited their American visas. Were they Jews, or the sons of anti-Hitler Protestants? We were too young to know to ask.

We did, however, dimly understand later that at the time the whole country was anxiously poised between Munich and the eventual outbreak of war. In the spring term 1939, men appeared and dug trenches at the back of the school and we lost part of the vegetable gardens and some grass tennis courts. In the summer holidays they had evidently returned and converted the trenches into two large air-raid shelters. By the time school started again war had been declared and we were in the library being fitted with gas masks. Air Raid Precautions required us always to carry them over our shoulders in neat brown boxes showing our names. One of us, A R Priestley, labelled his simply 'ARP'. But he was smart like that, even when bigger.

Jim, living in South London, had been able to go camping to Allhallows-on-Sea in Kent in the summer holidays of 1938, when he was eleven:

The campsite was ideally placed amongst farmland about five minutes' walk from the beach. A narrow country lane ran along one side, with the rest being fields and trees, a paradise for a boy of any age... We even had a boat trip to Southend on the Essex coast, where we stayed for the day and once again savoured those delicious spiral ice creams.

The following year:

Allhallows was growing into a mini seaside resort. There were a number of rides, including a scenic railway accompanied by the usual swindle stalls; they even had a part-time Punch and Judy man. Most of the fun was had on the beach, or in the sea, where I was grateful that Mother no longer knitted me woollen swimming trunks. Late in August, Bert arrived for his week's stay with us before we all returned to London. He had just settled down to his well-earned bottle of beer when the camp owner called at the tent to tell us that all campers had to leave by ten o'clock Sunday morning. The army was taking over the field for the preparation of coastal defences... Everyone was talking about a war that by now seemed inevitable.

Another John was five in 1939 and attended Primrose Hill School in London. He recalls preparations going on in the early summer:

My father joined the National Fire Service and they started using my school as a fire station. My father had a London taxi – the traditional black cab – with a pump on the back on a trailer: lots of taxis were commandeered and used like that, so that they could pump water on to fires. I have a photograph, taken after we children had been evacuated, of my dad and three or four other firemen standing on the steps of the school in front of the door that says 'Infants' above it. So he was stationed there, just by London Zoo. At the end of that road was a stables with about 200 horses in it – railway horses, because goods that were taken off the trains were still delivered by horse and cart; it got a direct hit during the war and a lot of the horses were killed.

For many who were small children in 1939, the declaration

of war, which happened in the school holidays, is a clear early memory. Paul was six:

The day war was declared we were on holiday in Exmouth. We were sitting on the beach – I think it was the day after the announcement – and my mamma suddenly said, 'I think we'd better pack up and go home.' So we did. That's all I remember of the occasion. I don't remember what the beach was like or how we got home, I just remember her saying that.

Ros was at home in Coulsdon, Surrey:

I remember it very clearly – I was in the garden, dancing to [Pietro Mascagni's] *Cavalleria rusticana* on our little gramophone. I used to do that a lot. I was ten and a half; I'd loved *Cavalleria rusticana* for as long as I could remember and I wanted to be a ballet dancer, so I suppose I was practising.

My mother came out of the house, because she'd just heard Chamberlain's announcement on the radio, and she said, 'You've got to come in. There's a war on.'

I didn't know what she was talking about, but I went in and then the air-raid siren went off. It was just for a moment or two – I don't know where the sound came from: perhaps it was on the radio and they were demonstrating the sound we'd have to listen out for, or perhaps the local ARP were having a practice. I don't remember being in the least frightened; it was a lovely day and I was just annoyed that there had been something on the radio that made my mother come out and get me inside.

Sylvia's father had been one of the founder members of the RAF, so was in it long before war broke out. In September 1939, he was stationed at Bircham Newton; the family was living in the nearby village of Heacham, on the Norfolk coast. Sylvia was twelve:

We'd known that war was going to happen. The prime minister was going to make a speech at eleven o'clock that Sunday morning and we had to be home to listen to the radio. Some friends and I had been for a walk round the village earlier in the morning and, to our great amusement, the village fire brigade was out having its photograph taken. It may have been total coincidence, or it may have been that some of them were going off to the war, but there they were, in full uniform, posing for their photograph.

I don't recall, as a child, people being frightened at the outbreak of war. I think everyone thought it would be over very quickly; but there was actually an air raid the very first day. The sirens went, as we'd been warned that they would, and we sat under the dining-room table for an hour or two. Then the all clear went, and that was that. So I'm not sure exactly what happened – I suppose someone saw something and thought it was a raid. Panicked, perhaps. But that was my first memory of war.

Connie in Liverpool was thirteen:

> I remember coming home from somewhere that Sunday morning and my mother saying, 'I've got terrible news. We're at war with Germany.' I just thought, 'So what?' – so casual, because at thirteen, in my day, you were still a little girl, nothing like as grown up as they are today. I took it all matter of fact. Then we started to get our ration books and gas masks, which we had to take everywhere we went, and I took it all for granted.

John in Yorkshire also recalls where he was:

> Chamberlain made the announcement on a Sunday morning, so I was one of many who first learned about it in church. To a certain extent I was ready for it because of hearing the grown-ups talking about their experiences of the Great War, and about what was happening in Europe. But even so I remember sitting in the pew and gasping. Then I expect we sang a hymn.

Nine-year-old David and his family lived in Beckenham, Kent, but they were on holiday in Wiltshire. On that fateful Sunday, the holiday was nearing its end and they were due to go home:

> My mother and father and a nearby farmer and his wife gathered round the radio to listen to Chamberlain. We children were playing outside. War was declared.

The farmer had a horse he'd brought back from the First World War – one of the famous 'war horses'. I remember thinking that it couldn't have been very long since the last war, since this horse was still alive, though when you're nine, twenty years seems quite a long time.

I know we had some ridiculously dangerous games that we played with the children of the village, including climbing through the haystacks. I don't know if this was a regular practice with haystacks in those days, but there was a hole right through the middle of the stack – for ventilation, perhaps, or to stop fires, I don't know. But the dare was to crawl right through the haystack, so you would be in complete darkness in the middle, and come out the other side. It was a summer game. After we'd finished playing, we went back towards the farm, where there was a road from Trowbridge. Two young men came along the road, shouting gleefully that there was a war on: they were about eighteen years old and I'm sure they would have been among the first to volunteer. There's a white horse carved into the Downs near there, and there were private planes practising over it. We could hear the drone of the aircraft. Some of the people piloting them were among the first to volunteer for the RAF.

We did hear from our parents that war had been declared and therefore, because gas, as well as high explosives, were expected in towns and our Aunt Rose down in Devon had warned us that 'the gutters would run with blood' and that type of thing, we were frightened that we shouldn't go home.

Our holiday had finished that weekend, so my father went back to London to work; my mother and we three children stayed on, but not at the same farm. My sister, who was the youngest, five or six, stayed somewhere with my mother. My brother and I were put into an alms house. The first thing we were told by the lady we were staying with was that she was giving us a good bedroom: 'This was my father's bedroom. He died in this room.' Not necessarily the most tactful thing to say to boys of nine and ten when war had just broken out. We were really a bit worried about staying in this house.

Meanwhile, Mum and Dad were industriously arranging for us to go to stay with relatives in South Devon, near Newton Abbot, so we only had to stay in that room for a few days.

Like thousands of others, we stayed away only a few weeks. London and other cities were not annihilated; no gas bombs were dropped. This was the period of the Phoney War – basically, nothing happened on the home front. So we went back to Beckenham.

There had been an official evacuation from the London area, but Beckenham, which was just across the border into Kent, was designated 'neutral'. We weren't in sufficient danger to be evacuated, but we weren't expected to take anybody in.

But less than a mile away, in Sydenham, which fell within the London County Council area, the streets were devoid of children. There may have been some Kindertransport children, moved there to escape from the Nazis, but no local children at all. It was completely quiet.

Bridget, aged four, was also away from home when the announcement came:

We lived in Wembley Park, a nice sort of Enid Blyton suburb in those days, but when war broke out, we were on holiday in Llandudno, not knowing it was going to start. I remember the blackout starting – we went to the cinema and when we came out, it was pitch-black. I can still remember the shock of that. We must have come home a few days later, because I can remember our garage being used to fill sandbags. And I remember getting my gas mask, which because I was little was like Mickey Mouse. Lots of small children had those. I suppose they thought we'd put them on more happily if it was like dressing up. It certainly had ears and a nose. Even so, it was horrid, but if you went to school without it, you were sent home to get it.

Gas masks – never needed – were a feature of everyone's war; the fear was that there would be gas attacks, as there had been in the First World War. By September 1939, 38 million masks had been issued. Even babies had to have them. Shirley remembers:

My youngest sister was born in 1938, so when war broke out she was just a year old and too small for a conventional gas mask; she had to be put into a sort of canvas suit, which fastened round her bottom like a nappy. Then there was a sort of helmet like a bubble on her head. She screamed and screamed when she was put into this contraption. I remember my parents agreeing that it was better for her not to wear it, even if the rest of us had to wear ours. Fortunately, that was never put to the test. But we children used to put them on and pretend to be pigs: we went 'Honk, honk', which sounds quite pig-like if you do it with a gas mask on.

Unless they were pretending to be pigs, nobody liked gas masks. Audrey is one of many who remembers how unpleasant they were:

We had to test them periodically and the smell of rubber was awful. You felt really claustrophobic.

And Irvine recalls that even if you had your gas mask with you, you wouldn't necessarily feel safe:

At school we were issued with gas masks in cardboard boxes with a string to hang them over our shoulder. Soon there came another worry – that the gas masks weren't safe. An extra green filter was taped on the end of each one because no one knew which gas the Germans would use.

Beryl, only two in 1939, had a worse experience than most:

It's lucky that I never had to wear a gas mask except for practice, because I turned out to be allergic to rubber. When I started wearing plimsolls for school, the soles of my feet got covered in spots and I had to wear something else. So goodness knows what would have happened to my face if we'd had a gas attack.

Gas attacks and bombing may not have started overnight, but the blackout did. Jean, evacuated from Portsmouth to the Isle of Wight two days before war was declared, remembers what a difference it made:

You had to black out your windows so that if you turned on a light indoors, nothing showed outside. Some people blocked them partly with paper and card round the edges and had thick curtains across, but you were never allowed to show a flash of light outside. There were Air Raid Wardens who came and checked and it was a bad offence if you did show light. Because the light would show where a town was, so when the bombers came in they could see where to bomb. So you tried to hide as much as possible. Car headlights were dimmed, too; road signs were taken down, so that if we were invaded they wouldn't know their way around, which was a bit stupid because all the road names were on the manhole covers and places like that, but the actual road signs were all taken down.

There were no streetlights, so if you went out you had to have a torch and you even had to be careful how much light you had from that and how you shone it. Lighting up the town was very, very strictly forbidden.

They also cut a whopping great chunk out of all the piers along the South Coast. I remember the one at Shanklin, on the Isle of Wight, which they later took down because it presumably wasn't worth repairing. The idea was, again if we were invaded, that the big ships could come in to the end of the pier, but then they wouldn't be able to land their troops or vehicles or whatever.

Tony in Luton has another memory of street lighting:

We had gas lights in the street and I remember the gasman coming round every night to light them. In perhaps the early and late summer – it was getting dark about eight o'clock – we kids used to follow him around and watch him do it. He had a pole with a hook on the end; hanging out the bottom of the light were two chains. One was always longer than the other and he used to hold the pole up and hook it into the shorter chain – that was 'off'. Then he'd pull it down, open the cage and use the hook to pull a little lever down. It would spark and that would set the gas mantle alight. He'd close the door and go on to the next one. We had three in our street, lighting about forty houses.

I assume in the morning he came round and turned them off, though I don't remember seeing him. I'd have been getting ready to go to school, because it was light by that time. And in the middle of summer we'd have been in bed before he came, because it didn't get dark till much later.

The thing that made the light work was a gas mantle. Gas mantles survived for a long time; we used to have them in our caravan twenty years later. They were like stretchy knitted bags, a bit like the toe of a sock, but made from asbestos. Nobody knew back then that asbestos was unhealthy. You had to be very careful with it, because it was held together with a sort of lacquer and once it had been lit, you only had to knock it and the whole thing would shatter. So the lamplighter had a very delicate job.

And then of course there was the blackout. If they knew there was going to be an air raid, or thought there might be, he didn't come round and the streets stayed dark. We didn't get raids every night, so if the lamplighter didn't come, that was an indication to expect trouble.

As another safety measure, the British government produced two types of shelter. The Anderson, named after the Lord Privy Seal Sir John Anderson, who had been entrusted with the task of preparing the country for air raids, was made of panels of galvanised steel and designed to be half-buried in the garden or some other outside space. These were issued free to the many people who earned less than five pounds a week and sold for seven pounds to the better-off. Accommodating up to about six people and often shared with neighbours, they tended to be cold and damp, even in summer, and were much disliked, although at the height of the Blitz many people slept in them night after night.

In addition to the Anderson there was the indoor Morrison shelter, named after Herbert Morrison, the Minister for Home Security. Seventy-five centimetres (two feet six inches) high and about the size of a small double bed, it had a mattress base, wire-meshed sides and a flat, heavy steel top. Many house-proud women disliked these, too, and covered theirs with a cloth, placed a vase of flowers on top of it and used it as a table. Shirley remembers:

> We were delivered with an Anderson shelter, and most of the neighbours were, too, because I remember furious diggings in people's back gardens. It was three strips of corrugated metal and a few screws. You had to dig a pit and put the metal over it, so when there was a raid you were half underground. Lots of people covered theirs with earth and planted cabbages on top. My mother hated it because it was so damp – the London clay soil didn't help – and getting four children out of bed and into the shelter in the middle of the night was a terrible trial.

Brenda's father was one of those who integrated his shelter into the garden:

> My father had been a nurseryman, so he was a keen gardener and grew lots of vegetables. You'd go out into the garden through the kitchen, down a little pathway,

with a rockery on either side and then you'd get to the shed and the vegetable garden and the Anderson shelter, with a vegetable patch on top. It came as a prefab – the council must have come and installed it and they screwed all the parts together. It stayed there for years after the war – one of my daughters remembers seeing it when she was a little girl, visiting her grandparents, and that would have been in the 1960s.

Tony's family shared an Anderson shelter:

We didn't have one in our garden, but the people in the next street, whose garden backed on to ours, did. A man called Fred, who lived with his mother. My mum and dad were friendly with them and I remember Fred and my dad cutting out a bit of the fence between us and making a little gate, so if we needed to go into a shelter at night, we used to go through there. When he first put it in, Fred also brought some sawdust home, and he and my dad mixed up buckets of flour and water into a paste and painted the inside of the shelter with it. Then they threw the sawdust on to the walls and it would stick. A couple of days later, they did the same thing, to make a thicker layer: it soundproofed the shelter a bit and meant it wasn't quite so cold.

There were benches along the wall of the shelter and there used to be my mum, Fred's mum, the lady who lived next door to them and me, aged about five or six; the men would be outside, looking around. They never shut the door – you weren't allowed to, you always had to keep it ajar: it was the same if you were in the cupboard under the stairs. The idea was that if there was an explosion, the door could be blocked and you'd never get out, but if it was ajar, you had a chance of escaping.

We didn't have a Morrison shelter – we used to sit in the cupboard under the stairs, because there was nothing above them, only the tiles and the roof, whereas if you'd been in a downstairs room you had the risk of the whole top storey falling on you. My mum had a cylinder hoover that had a big wooden box and it lived in that cupboard, so that's what we sat on if we had to go in there.

We didn't have many daylight raids, but Commer Karrier, a local firm that made vehicle parts, was bombed during the day and the shockwaves blew all the plates off the dresser in our kitchen. I can also remember sitting in class and the sirens going off and the teacher saying, 'Come on, we have to go down the shelter.' The shelter was just like a concrete building underneath the playground, with concrete steps down to it. It was fenced-off, and we used to have to go down the steps and sit on benches along the side until they gave us the all clear.

The sirens were dotted all over everywhere – I think they must have been on the factories and perhaps on the fire station, because sometimes the siren went off on the edge of town and sometimes it was down in the centre.

According to the government, trouble could be expected from other sources than bombs and gas attacks. In September 1939, there were some 80,000 potential enemy aliens living in Britain. Never mind that a substantial number of them were refugees from the Nazi regime; Germans and Austrians alike were called before a tribunal and subjected to what might today be called a risk assessment. As a result, they were categorised as:

- A, high-risk: about 600 people, who were interned immediately;
- B, doubtful: about 6,500, to be supervised and have their movements restricted;
- C, no security risk: the rest. About three-quarters of these, the vast majority of them Jewish, were acknowledged as refugees from Nazi oppression.

Category C aliens were left at liberty until, in 1940, the increased fear of an invasion also increased the fear (or paranoia) that anyone of German, Austrian and by then also Italian origin was likely to be a spy. This led to many more people being taken into custody. Churchill's policy, though it's not clear if he actually used these words, is frequently summarised as 'collar the lot'.

Sybilla was born in Ealing, West London, in 1923, to a German father and an English mother. Her father had lived and worked in England before the First World War, was interned during it and subsequently repatriated to Germany. Sometime in the 1930s he and his family returned to Ealing, 'probably because Mother saw what was coming in Germany'. But although he was married to an Englishwoman, he didn't become a naturalised British citizen. In 1939 the family was running a 'ham and beef dealer' – a sort of delicatessen:

On 2 September 1939 (a Saturday), the shop was particularly busy. There was much talk of children being evacuated; parents wanted to make sandwiches for their journey. Two men came in and asked if they could have a word with Father. They identified themselves as police officers and more or less said, 'Come with us.' My father asked, 'Where to?' and their reply was, 'Can't say yet.' He was allowed to pack a small case, Mother made him a sandwich and then he was taken, to the astonishment of customers, to a waiting car and driven away. Needless to say, my mother, elder sister and I were very apprehensive. However, Mother remained calm.

Later that afternoon, early evening, my sister visited the police station in the High Street and was informed that, together with other German nationals, he had been taken to Olympia, Earl's Court. We learned later that this included even Jewish refugees and merchant seamen. I recall my father saying, just before he was taken away, '*Das verdammtest Mann!*' [that most damned of men], meaning Hitler, of course. Father deliberately held no political views, and for that matter neither did my mother. From Olympia, my father was taken, together with other internees, to a holiday camp at Seaton, Devon, and then to the Isle of Man. Then Mother was worried because we had heard that from there some internees had been taken to Canada.

Mother moved heaven and earth to get Father released – she was concerned about his health, as he was in his sixties. She visited councillors and our MP, and he was allowed home. When the situation worsened after the so-called 'Phoney War', he was re-interned at Lingfield racecourse. When he was finally allowed home for good he did not work in the shop again – 'in case someone misconstrued something' he said.

Mother received some hate mail, which she tore up and binned with contempt. There was virtually no animosity towards us from the public. During rationing, customers registered with particular shops and ours remained very loyal.

Martin's school had been evacuated to Westward Ho! in Devon, where he found himself with some well-known neighbours:

At the top of the hill, up which we went on cross-country runs and which overlooked the village and pebble ridge, a small holiday camp had been taken over by the Army Pioneer Corps unit formed for non-combatant internees of German, Austrian, Italian and Russian nationality who were unable or unwilling to repatriate. Among these were Coco the Clown, who was Russian by birth, and several musicians, including a famous violinist.

Martin doesn't remember the name of that violinist, but two musicians who were later half of the world-famous Amadeus Quartet, the violinist Norbert Brainin and viola player Peter Schidlof, Jewish refugees from Austria, met while interned on the Isle of Man. Fellow inmates included the future publisher André Deutsch, Walter Freud, grandson of Sigmund (both also Austrian Jews) and Charles Forte, who went on to found the catering and hotel group that became Trust House Forte – he had been born in Italy but moved to Scotland when he was four.

Throughout the war, Rose kept up a correspondence from Bromley, Kent, with her married sister in Switzerland. On 12 June 1940, after writing about what was happening in Europe, she had this to report:

Here, all aliens have been cleared away 20 miles from the coast (Dad says Father Bathbrick has to go, although he is Dutch and what is going to happen to their farm, etc., we don't know). There are many barricades on roads, etc. and Lil passed a great many of all descriptions on her way back from the coast over the weekend.

On Monday evening, a few minutes after six, Mum rang up and told me that Musso[lini] had declared war and then rang off quickly to hear the rest of the news.

I don't know whether we have caught a spy or not, or a fifth columnist, but last night, when Lil took Bob [the family dog] over the way, she found a man in officer's uniform sketching (practically dark), so she scurried back and Mum phoned 999, got put through to Scotland Yard, gave particulars and in five or ten minutes, a police van came up and they got the man. Of course, he might be perfectly innocent, but on the other hand he might not, and it is better to be sure than sorry. Anyway, his actions were suspicious. I don't know whether we will hear anything else. Of course, over the way is very intriguing for certain people on account of works going on there, especially being an open space, and I dare say there are many suspicious characters who find their way there. The police had rifles, and Dad filled his revolver and went too, but met them coming back with the man, so he emptied his revolver again, and spent until 12 o'c talking.

A few days later:

By the way, our Spy turned out all right, his wife is a commandant in the W.A.A.Cs, his daughter also something in the Women's something or other, and his son an officer in the Army. He admitted it was very silly to sketch and he didn't have any animosity against the bloke who put him away, but he was an artist by profession, and when he saw some trees in a certain light, unthinkingly whipped out his notebook and sketched them. He nearly had a pink fit when he was collared. (We got all this from Clark the garage man.) So that is that.

Sylvia, moving around a lot because of her father's various RAF postings, found herself back in Norfolk, later in the war:

The schools were all full, because a lot of London schoolchildren had been evacuated to Norfolk. So instead of going back to the grammar school, which didn't have any places, my younger sister and I went to a convent in Hunstanton, the next village along. For some extraordinary reason this was run by a German order of nuns. A lot of them were actually Germans and later in the war they were interned, but not while I was there. It seems extraordinary – the thinking behind it is quite difficult. But there was a fear of German spies dressing up as nuns – it would have been an easy form of disguise. It happened in *Dad's Army*, so I suspect that that sort of rumour was around in real life, too.

John, born in Germany in 1924, had escaped the Nazi regime with his dentist mother. They had spent some time with an uncle in Amsterdam but by 1939 were living in Cambridge. His education there was assisted by a lady named Greta Burkill, who was in charge of the local refugee committee and who is credited with having received 20,000 refugee children in East Anglia:

Mrs Burkill arranged to get me into Leys School at reduced fees. In my first term I couldn't speak any English, because I'd only been in England for six weeks and I'd done French at school – if I'd stayed in Holland another year I would have done English. I'd learned my first words on the boat from the Hook of Holland to Harwich – yes and no.

This was in 1937. I was thirteen and at school they were very kind to the little German boy. Then on my sixteenth birthday, I saw a policeman walking across the quad to the Headmaster's house, and I knew what was coming because another refugee had been interned on his sixteenth birthday and I knew they were coming for me. So I stopped writing the English essay I was writing – it was early summer and I was about to take the equivalent of GCSEs – and the policemen came. They were very nice, very polite. They took me home, told my mother to pack a suitcase for a few days and I was taken by car to Bury St Edmunds, to an army camp where I learned what a palliasse was – a mattress made out of straw. There were a lot of refugees from Cambridge University and I learned all about syphilis and that sort of thing because they were giving talks, lectures.

After I don't know exactly how long we were taken to Huyton, near Liverpool, to a new camp that had only just been finished. What they did was surround the existing houses – which were not even occupied at that time, they were quite new – with barbed wire, and the youngsters, like myself, were put in a tent in the garden, whereas the older people were put in a house. My house contained three people who subsequently became Fellows of the Royal Society: Max Perutz, the haemoglobin man; Hermann Lehmann, who was also a blood man, and a third who was an expert on potato viruses whose name I can't recall. They weren't FRSs at the time – they became FRSs later – but it was a very learned house.

From there one day we were taken by boat to Glasgow, or rather to the port of Glasgow, Greenock, and put on another boat, a Polish boat, and taken to Canada. This is all within a month or two of being interned. And there we were taken to a camp which again hadn't been quite finished yet, but we were quite relieved because food in Huyton was short and we were usually hungry, whereas at least in Canada there was enough food.

Then after about six months in Canada, during which time I learned to fell trees, because we had wood-burning stoves – we were quite near the American border but I don't think anyone ever tried to escape to America, which at that time wasn't in the war yet – after about six months, they began to realise that Churchill saying, 'Grab the lot, intern the lot' was really rather silly, because interning refugee Jewish people from Germany as potential enemies of the state – well, it was silly. So the Home Office sent a man along to interview us individually and I was given the choice of either being released in Canada, where I didn't know anybody, or going back home. So we sailed back home. And luckily, in these two convoys, nobody was torpedoed. So that policy was reversed.

With reference to the A, B and C categories of aliens, John observed:

The Cs were at the discretion of the local Chief Constable, who in his wisdom thought that my mother was safe to leave but that I was possibly – possibly – a danger.

CHAPTER 2

'I PLAYED WITH THE FROGS RATHER THAN GO TO SCHOOL'

Because it was widely believed that, once war was declared, bombing and invasion would follow almost immediately, the British government developed a policy for protecting the next generation: remove children from likely targets (industrial centres and ports) and keep them safely in the country until the danger was over. Under Operation Pied Piper, as it was called, entire schools were sent away, either to suitable buildings that had been requisitioned or to be billeted on schools in the designated areas. Accommodation for pupils and teachers alike was arranged in a haphazard way: trainloads of evacuees were met at the station, herded into the village hall and asked to hang around while willing locals came and chose the children they were prepared to take in. When, as generally happened, there were more evacuees than there were homes for them, unwilling locals had to be cajoled too.

Not every urban parent acquiesced in this scheme. Some refused to break up the family; some took the attitude that if they were going to die then they would all die together. Still others chose to take or send their children to relatives in the country. But whether or not they were part of Operation Pied Piper, evacuation took hundreds of thousands of children away from their homes and more often than not away from their parents, too.

Then came what became known as the Phoney War. For the first six months or so after war was declared, most of the 'action' was in mainland Europe and the British began to feel that the war would be over by Christmas or, when it wasn't, that it would somehow just go away. Some evacuee children were miserably homesick; some parents missed them unbearably. Whatever the reason, after a matter of only weeks or months, many parents simply took their children home again, in good time to be in London or Liverpool or Portsmouth for the Blitz. But some children stayed away for five years – seeing their parents anything from every weekend to once or twice or not at all. Some loved the experience and the introduction to country life; some were baffled by it; others were simply and deeply unhappy.

Gwen was attending Mary Datchelor's Girls' School, a 'well-known and respected' grammar school in South London. Aged thirteen in 1938, she was already conscious of the threat of war:

Nationally, some hoped war might be avoided by negotiation and concentrating on peace. Others, more realistic, realised it had become inevitable and preparations were begun.

It was seen that, this time, civilians would be involved, and safety and preservation of the next generation would be paramount. Plans were made to evacuate vital services, the Civil Service and city schools to rural areas.

Parents' meetings were held at school and mine came home with news of reassuring plans. A special haversack was purchased and filled with twenty essential items, mostly toilet goods, bought from a list supplied by school. The school number 'LCC H 70' was written indelibly on the backpack. Presumably 'H' stood for higher education.

It was midsummer and I went with my parents to Cornwall for our annual two weeks' holiday. Even in a small fishing village – Port Isaac – civil defence organisations were being established.

Back home, Gwen continues, a year passed with an increasing sense of foreboding. Then, on Friday morning, 1 September 1939…

…all girls taking part in the school's evacuation assembled in the hall. (A good number stayed behind or went privately to relatives in Britain and the Colonies.)

We wore our school uniform, our gas masks in cardboard boxes slung across our chests, our own name and school number 'H 70' on tie-on labels and carried our haversacks containing the vital twenty items from the official list and a few personal relics we could squeeze in – and of course our emergency rations. (What importance and connotation that word was to assume in the next years!)

Earlier, I had said goodbye to Father from home. Strange, for usually we walked to the local station together. Then I gave my bedroom its last look for a long while, cuddled our tabby cat and said goodbye to Grandpa.

So, a new era began. Things were never the same again. The whole world was about to change.

The evacuation of schoolchildren was a typically British operation, taken on in faith, relying on people's goodwill. To transport children from five years old upward to be billeted in unknown homes, initially in unnamed destinations, would be unthinkable now.

Possibly such secrecy was accepted because war was imminent and thus folks acquiesced in the national interest. Future uncertainty was unquestioned now and to send the children to safety away from anticipated bombing, as in Europe, was a sheet-anchor. Faith in schools and teachers was deep and evacuation under the wings of the school was accepted gratefully. No one was lost. We too were on our mettle – this was war and we were British, we cooperated and complied quietly.

We set off from school, two by two, in a forlorn crocodile, up the hill, Grove Lane, to Denmark Hill station, where our relatives were waiting to see us off. My mother and two aunts were among them. There weren't many dry eyes, but it was the grown-ups who cried rather than the children. We were too astonished at the strangeness. My mother managed not to cry but be reassuring and supportive to me. She always said tears did not help, but I expect she was pretty touchy to live with that weekend.

After six months in Ashford, Kent, the Mary Datchelor girls were forced to move again:

Early summer 1940
Spring joys and the Phoney War were soon to pass. France was being overrun, would soon capitulate, and the German forces and coastal guns across the English Channel would be too close for safety. So we had to commence our second evacuation. Soon we were entrained for an unknown destination in South Wales among the slate roofs and chimney stacks of the steel works. Again, we boarded the train with our luggage, gas masks, inevitable labels (LCC H 70) and packs of sandwiches. We boarded the train at Ashford and remained on it all day. The convoluted journey cleverly arranged by Southern and South Western railways and skilful use of points continued to take us through the southern stations to London Paddington and then south-west without disembarking. Some said later that, due to an administrative error, we were sent to Wales, rather than Sussex, where one neighbouring boys' school was received.

The unknown destination turned out to be Llanelli, Carmarthenshire, where Gwen remained for three years. Schooling continued as best it could:

Girls not taking Lower School Certificate (sixteen) or Higher School Certificate (eighteen) assembled for lessons somehow. Books and equipment arrived, but such an impromptu move must have been a nightmare for the teachers. To plan a timetable in various strange buildings, without correct materials to support a curriculum, and assorted groups of pupils, must be the ultimate challenge. In London, we had been organised in the customary age groups and in sets for ability. Now an incomplete staff – some had not come to Wales – had to cope with an administratively awkward school roll. But we gathered steam and felt an identity…

'Mary Datchelor in Wales' was established and the school day began with corporate prayers as usual. In London, we had a fine hall with stained-glass windows over a platform, an organ, chairs inscribed with the donor's name and a balcony at the back, under which was a replica of the Elgin Marbles mounted on the wall. Having held a staff meeting previously, the headmistress led in a procession of the staff; senior mistresses sat beside her on the platform and we sang a hymn from our specially printed 'Datchelor hymnal'…

In Llanelli, a very much reduced school took part in a similar ritual, trying to maintain the spirit of the daily assembly. Of the 347 girls who went to Ashford on the first evacuation, possibly half remained. For our hall we used the crypt of Church of England St Alban's, which was across the road from some of our classrooms. The customary Order of Service was maintained; our school organ was replaced with a piano, played by girls taking the VI form music course (of which I was one), and we used our Datchelor hymnal.

And so, in unfamiliar circumstances, the familiar routine was established. There was some stability, even security, from the thought that we would surely remain here 'for the duration', and had better make the best of it.

Kate was another Mary Datchelor pupil. Aged sixteen when she was sent to Llanelli, she described it in a letter home as 'ever such a queer town':

It is much bigger than Ashford and we cannot find our way about so easily. They have trolley buses instead of ordinary buses. I expect it would be a prosperous holiday resort if it were not for the steel works near the beach. It is not safe for bathing here as there is a river estuary and there are queer currents, but the school are going to organise bathing parties further round the coast.

Sheila from the East End of London was also evacuated to Wales:

I remember the little label I had stuck on me and the box with my gas mask. We were sent to a place near Mountain Ash and stayed with a miner and his wife. I went to school there, but most of the children spoke Welsh and I was so uncomfortable with that that I kept running out of the school. Beside the houses there was a cobbled alleyway and I remember watching the little frogs playing on the wet pipes, the drainpipes that came out of people's houses. So I played with the frogs rather than go to school.

For Brenda, in a Hampshire village, it was the evacuees who seemed 'foreign':

I had several aunties living in the village. Two of them took in evacuees from London and they seemed different from us – it's difficult to pinpoint in what sense. I won't say we took the mickey out of them, but we didn't quite see them as 'one of us'. They just were different: we lived a proper country life and they came from a large city, so it must have been very different for them as well. They spoke differently, too.

Ellen and Jean, sisters from the East End, had a difficult start as evacuees, but eventually settled down happily. Ellen recalls:

I was just coming up for five – I turned five in October after the war started. My sister was two years older and we were evacuated with our school and another one from the same area, from the East End to Croxley Green, near Watford. When we got there, it was most strange; we all assembled on this big common and from there we were given our instructions and divided up as to where we were to go.

At first we stayed with a family, but after a while they moved and we were transferred to another woman. We were unhappy with her, so they transferred us again. This time we went to a couple we enjoyed being with. Then they grew too old to look after us, so we were transferred to yet another family – that was four different homes in six years. That last family was very kind to us, though. We got to be fond of them and kept in touch for many years. We were lucky in that Watford isn't that far from London, so our mother could come to visit every weekend.

Because we were so young, it seemed as if we really were in the country: there were all sorts of things we hadn't seen before – green fields, the common, which was a huge place where we used to play. I suppose the common was always in our life because we enjoyed it so much. From there we could also go to the side woods, down the hill, through the watercress beds to the river, where we would catch tiddlers and play. Another memory I have of the common is that the farmer would come out with a big basket of cherries, which all the children would gather round and take.

There was a wood, where we could play for the whole day: in and out and round about, running around, hide and seek, that sort of thing. If you went right through the woods you came to a gravel pit, but we were a bit frightened of it and tended to avoid it.

It was all very unusual for us, compared with what we were used to in London. We did go to school, but what I remember most about that time is exploring and playing in the summer. We learned to love the countryside. It was idyllic in many ways, but of course in other ways it wasn't.

In one sense Bob actually benefited from being away from home:

I was evacuated from Liverpool to North Wales, near Bethesda. I had to walk to and from school, three miles each way every day. I dare say I was better fed in the country than I would have been in the city, too. At the end of the war I was so fit that when I went back to my old school in Liverpool, I broke all the athletics records.

Paul's school was evacuated from one grand building to another:

During the summer of 1940 I went off to prep school in Kent, which was a prime target for bombing. It was a lovely old Jacobean house, but after one term we were evacuated to the Welsh borders, west of Shrewsbury – very wet and very cold – to a large baronial mansion. The young son of the house was one of the pupils at the school, but I don't know what happened to the parents. The building had simply been requisitioned and they had to go elsewhere. I think we looked after it rather well, unlike the place in Kent that we were evacuated from: it was taken over by some of our allies and entirely vandalised.

Lots of people were evacuated to grand places: someone we knew was sent from school in North Wales to Chatsworth House in Derbyshire, where the State Drawing Room was made into a dormitory. There's a painting by Edward Halliday called 'Chatsworth in Wartime', showing the girls in their magnificent sleeping quarters: our friend Jean is the one brushing her hair in the foreground.

Where I was, food was very short and it was awful, too. We had a lot of rabbit, which I've only recently come round to liking again. And prunes, which I couldn't abide. There were a lot of prunes. There's nothing I like better now than rabbit stewed with prunes, but it was a long time before I could stomach either. The saving grace was that there was a wonderful walled fruit and vegetable garden. Some of us boys used to go down in the middle of the night and eat all the raspberries. The headmaster said one day, 'I can't make this out. We have this lovely fruit which ripens, and it all disappears.' He also told us not to pick the wild garlic: 'You'll smell horrible,' he said.

We had a number of nocturnal ventures – I don't know why, but a group of us just used to sneak out. The school had a big baronial hall with a sort of stage at one end, and under the stage was a trapdoor. It led down a passage which came out somewhere in the garden. The trapdoor was out of bounds, of course, and the passage was very narrow: you had to crawl along it. It was all enormously exciting. It's also how I got keen on bird-watching, and particularly owls. I've been very fond of owls ever since.

During these outings we saw lots of flashing lights all over the countryside. I don't know what they were – defences of some sort, I expect – but we were all convinced that it was the Germans about to attack us. But it was fun, not serious at all.

I remember trying to make cheese once. That was not very successful. I think we were encouraged to have a go at more or less anything, to keep us amused or out of mischief. There was quite a large farm attached to this place and they had cattle, so we would have had access to plenty of milk.

It was an amazing place, that house. It had everything except a swimming pool, because nobody did have swimming pools in those days. But we used to go and swim in the River Severn, which was very dirty and muddy. You wouldn't be allowed to do that now. In front of the house was a long, sweeping drive, with an entrance on either side, and bang in the middle there were three tennis courts. Tennis was a great thing there – they had tournaments with local schools and took it very seriously. I think the headmaster's wife was keen on tennis; she was also very keen on the cinema. We used to have films in the evening. There was a series about Dr Syn, which took place on Romney Marshes – they were about smuggling. Then there were all those patriotic films, like *In Which We Serve* – compulsory viewing. We had a wonderful movie projector, which kept on breaking down, of course, as they did in those days.

Life was very quiet up there – one didn't feel part of anything very much. There was no bombing at all.

Martin, aged sixteen at the start of the war, found life at Westward Ho! on the whole enjoyable:

I was mainly responsible for starting a hockey team and an ATC [Air Training Corps], as an alternative to the school OTC [Officers' Training Corps]. Another boy and I also started a Sea Scout patrol, the main objective of which was to sail on the waters of the estuary formed by the confluence of the rivers Taw and Torridge. With the help of a retired admiral in Appledore, an old whaler was given to us, and in this we learned the arts of sailing and rowing.

As part of our 'war effort' I had at regular intervals to cycle in the early hours to the cliff edges south of Westward Ho! and gaze out to sea, searching for stray sea-mines and other dangers. Apart from the agony of thawing fingers, it was not an unpleasant duty. Other memories are of crossing Pebble Ridge at spots marked to avoid the mines buried in the pebbles, and swimming in the sea before breakfast as an alternative to PT on the lawn. It seems extraordinary that we were allowed – even encouraged – to go down to the beach when there were mines all around. Sadly, I remember several local dogs that failed to read the warning notices.

Margaret was also sixteen and living in Walthamstow, in Essex:

I'd just done my School Certificate and was enrolled at a college to do secretarial studies with French. But the day the term was due to start was the day of the big evacuation. The college was evacuating to the Midlands, so off I went with them. When we got there, we were met by the local Scouts and taken to a church hall, where people who were going to take in evacuees came and chose a child.

In the end there were about half a dozen of us whom nobody wanted, because we were teenagers. So the billeting officer took us round – it was like a slave market, really – knocking on doors and saying, 'Will you have this girl?' In the end, a lady offered to have me. She had two boys of her own, aged about eleven and thirteen, and she was very kind and we got on very well. In the event I only stayed with her for a couple of months because my mother wasn't terribly well and my father thought I ought to come home. So having been evacuated in order to be kept safe, I was back well in time for the Blitz.

Not all evacuations were formal. Billy's parents, Scots living in London, simply took him home to Bathgate in West Lothian:

I remember bringing a paper home from school one day, a note from the teacher. It must have been at the end of the summer term, in July or so, 1939. My mother read it and discovered that I was to be evacuated to Wales, with the rest of the school. That put the clinchers on it: my parents, who weren't really happy in London, decided we would return to Scotland. My mother and I went first, while my father organised things, such as sending our furniture after us. My mother had money saved up to put a deposit on a house, but moving some of our things and putting the rest in store took most of it. So that was the end of my mother's pipe dream. She had ambitious plans, but the war snuffed an awful lot of it.

After a short stay with Billy's grandfather, the family moved into their own house:

This house – in a two-storey tenement called Prentice's Buildings – had a scullery and an inside toilet!

Bathgate was a completely different world from my London experience. Prentice's Buildings had a piece of land next to it that was owned by the local borough. Half of it was very stony and wouldn't have been any good for gardening, but the other half was ploughed up and turned into plots where we were being incited to 'Dig for Victory' – what today would be called allotments. Our tenement consisted of two buildings separated by a close and there was a bit of back lawn that was the 'drying green'. This was in the days before washing machines and so on, so you had an outside wash house and you needed somewhere to dry the washing. But one of the buildings was set back a bit from the road – it had a lawn in front and the people who lived there dug up their lawn, too, and used it for vegetables. That was going on all over the place – people sacrificing their gardens and turning them into a place where they could grow food. I can remember helping my father to dig the turf out and laying it like a dyke or a wall round our particular plot. Everybody did that: it defined each plot and created paths to walk on between them.

The Wee Mair infant school to which I was sent had no air-raid shelters, so when we had an air-raid drill we were told to run home, touch the house door and then (as it was only a drill) come back to school. Jean Meikle lived upstairs in the next Prentice's Building. As I was nearest to school I should have been first back; there were no prizes for being first, but in our child minds it seemed a desirable goal. Jean and I would run down Milburn Road neck and neck till she got to the close between the buildings. I had a little further to go to touch my front door. She cheated and only touched the side of the close, instead of running round and up the stairs to her own door, so she got back first. I wasn't pleased.

Like Billy's parents, Brenda's wanted to keep the family together as best they could:

I was seven when war broke out, with a brother of nine and a sister of twelve. We were all at different schools in London and my parents were worried that if we were evacuated, we would be separated. So they decided that

Mum would take us back to Aberdeen, where she and Dad came from. Dad worked for the Press Association, so he would have to stay behind and work, but Mum and the three of us went to live with my grandmother and two unmarried aunts in their house in Aberdeen.

We stayed there for 'the duration' and my father used to come up for two weeks every summer, to spend his holidays with us and enjoy a game or two of golf. I missed him terribly, but the thing that makes me feel dreadful to this day is that we left London on Saturday, 26 August, just a week before war broke out. In all the anxiety and bustle – and saying goodbye to this lovely man whom we might never see again – we completely forgot that it was his birthday. Whether he remembered or not, I'll never know, but it didn't occur to any of the rest of us until we were on the train, steaming north, and it was too late to do anything about it.

Brian, aged four, initially stayed at home with his parents near Ewell in suburban Surrey:

One of my most vivid memories of those early wartime summers is of a German fighter plane – a Messerschmitt Bf 109 – hurtling over the rooftops in broad daylight with smoke pouring out of it and the pilot struggling vainly to extricate himself before it crashed in the park at the top of our road. Moments later, an RAF Hurricane flew overhead, waggling its wings in a victory roll as everyone rushed out of their houses to cheer and wave.

By then I had become used to the banshee wail of the air-raid sirens and the nightly bombing raids that left bright shards of shiny shrapnel to be picked up in the road on my way to school. But then one night the bombs came closer to home and blew down the ceiling on top of me as I slept. That same morning, while we were having breakfast, a delayed-action bomb went off in the neighbouring street, blew the kitchen door off its hinges and sent it flying across the room.

For my parents that was the last straw, and so, clutching my gas mask and a suitcase of clothes and favourite books, I was packed off to the safety of a thirty-five-acre farm deep in the Cornish countryside near Bude. There I lived for the next two years in an unchanged world of oil lamps and stone-flagged floors, with an outside toilet full of spiders and a well from which water was hauled up in a wooden bucket.

For some reason I have never discovered, I never went to school. Instead, I roamed wild through the fields or else helped out with the day-to-day running of the farm, collecting the eggs laid by the free-range hens, feeding slops to the family pig, learning how to call in the six cows for milking and digging up potatoes until my back felt as if it would break. Although I was there for two years and collected eggs nearly every day, I don't remember ever eating one – the family was very poor and I suppose all the eggs had to be sold.

Winters were a blur of mist, when owls called in the long dark evenings spent huddled around the kitchen range for warmth. Spring was a miracle of bluebell woods and flowering hedge banks from which (unforgivable in retrospect) I once picked an armful of purple orchids.

But summers are what I remember most, waking early to the twitter of swallows under the eaves and going out to set gin traps for the rabbits that were a regular part of our diet. I don't remember being shocked by the cruelty. Instead, I just accepted it as part of my new life, despatching them with a blow behind the head and then plucking out their entrails, although I now recoil at the thought and was glad to see gin traps consigned to history.

Like all small boys, despite those weekly rabbit stews I was perpetually hungry, stealing carrots from the fields to eat raw, gorging myself on windfall apples and feasting on blackberries until my hands were stained purple.

The Atlantic coast was only three miles away, but I never saw the sea, until one memorable day when everyone for miles around hurried down to the beach after word had spread of a shipwreck. Apparently, a ship laden with supplies for American troops had been torpedoed and its cargo had been washed up on the sands, free for the taking.

Like the wreckers of old, the Cornish reverted to type and we joined the throng who were already picking their way through the packing cases bobbing in the surf. One farmer waded in up to his waist to retrieve a large wooden box in the hope that it contained

Bourbon or tins of tobacco, only to find it was full of wet toilet rolls.

By comparison I did far better, gathering a haul of tinned pineapple and a whole box of spearmint chewing gum. But I'm afraid I paid for my sins as I ate so much pineapple followed by a whole tin of peanuts that I was violently sick that evening.

In the days that followed, the police scoured the surrounding countryside in the hope of recovering the wreck's ill-gotten spoils. I was told that as part of their search they even cut hayricks in half, but nothing was ever found.

My long Cornish exile finally came to an end when I fell out of the farm cart and broke my arm. After being sent up-country to Exeter hospital to have my arm encased in plaster, I was collected by my parents and taken back home. By then I had acquired such a broad Cornish accent that even my mother found it hard to understand me. But once I was back with my friends it soon fell away and I returned to school none the worse for my adventures, apart from a complete inability to understand mathematics that has remained with me to this day.

Beryl's evacuation also came once the war was well underway, as a result of the London Blitz:

I was about five when I was evacuated to Castleton in Lancashire, after we were bombed out of our house in

Fulham. As luck had it, there was a brick shelter where we could go, in the road, as well as an Anderson shelter in the garden, and for some reason that day we'd gone into the brick shelter. If we hadn't, I wouldn't be here now, because our garden and the Anderson were bombed. The house and all our furniture were badly damaged, but all I really remember about it is that we had been out shopping earlier in the day and Mum had bought me a smart new coat. It was hanging in the wardrobe and I remember being in the shelter and being much more worried about what was going to happen to my coat than about anything else. Mum assured me it would be fine – and she was right, it was!

But I do remember coming out of the shelter and seeing glass everywhere: that was awful. We had a cat at the time and it had run off. Dad managed to catch it, but it was so terrified, it scratched him and he had to let it go. What became of it, I just don't know.

Because we couldn't go home, we went to a local school, where they had camp beds set up and people who'd been bombed out could stay for a little while. Then somehow someone found us a new house a few streets away: it wasn't such a nice house, but it was liveable and we were lucky to have it. My mother lived there until the 1970s – most of that time with no inside loo.

Anyway, it was decided that I should be sent away somewhere safe; why Castleton was chosen, I don't know, but there must have been a lot of children in the same position. I remember a crowd of us getting off the train and being taken to the village hall, sitting there while all the local people who were willing to take in a child came and picked who they wanted. I was literally the last to be chosen. I just had to sit there, by myself, wondering what was going to happen to me. The organisers must have gone out and coerced a few more people into volunteering, because the couple who did eventually take me in were older – more like my grandparents' age than my parents' – and they may not have been an obvious choice at first.

But as it turned out, they were lovely. They'd never had any children and I was treated very well. A friend of mine went to the same village, to a couple of ladies who weren't very nice to her, so she went home, but I stayed for two or three years and I was very happy. There was a family next door and I made friends with their children. There were lovely fields all around, where we used to go and play hide and seek. I went to school up a cobbled lane and one day, coming home, skipping, I fell and came home covered in blood. The lady was so concerned – 'Oh, what have you done?' – they couldn't have been better, really. Well, not as good as my parents, but they did look after me very well. They even wanted to adopt me, but my mother wouldn't have that!

Mum used to come and visit, and she would stay a couple of days. I remember one time she brought me a doll – a very realistic-looking one, like a real baby – with several outfits she had made. Lovely clothes, at a time when new clothes were difficult to get, so this was a very well-dressed doll! As for what *I* wore, Mum used to send dresses for me sometimes, but in all the time I was in Castleton, I can't remember ever going out shopping for clothes.

Separation from parents was, of course, one of the hardest things for evacuated children. With transport difficult, money short and holidays no more than a week a year for many working people, even short distances could be insuperable. John was only thirty miles from home in London, but saw his parents only once or twice in five years:

I have a photograph of them that was taken at the house I was living in, with Mr and Mrs Higgins; another time, my mother came on her own for a fortnight and stayed in a pub in Eton and I went and stayed with her. But she was working – she was a shorthand/typist at the Ministry of Food – and that was probably the first holiday she'd had all through. There was also the family business – sculptors' tools and materials – which had been blitzed twice, so my parents were trying to run that in the latter part of the war.

My dad did get down one time when I was at the Higgins', near the beginning of the war, and he made some shutters for them. They had a wooden frame with very thick black roofing felt over, which you pushed closed from outside for the blackout. Because of course the blackout was very serious – if you showed a light, all

hell was let loose. We used my dad's shutters all through
the war.

Norm, living in Portsmouth, was old enough to join the
Navy when war broke out. He served on HMS *Anson* in the
Russian convoy run. At home, he had four younger siblings
and an important naval port was no place for them:

Sister Marjorie was thirteen years old, sister Hazel eleven
and the twins, Stan and Vera, just six. When they were
told what being evacuated meant, they burst into tears.
They were to go to the tiny village of Swanmore, a
stone's throw from Portsmouth – for how long, nobody
seemed to know or care. They paraded one day at
Gosport station and, as Marjorie often said afterwards,
'It was so difficult not to cry!'

Arriving at Swanmore meant parading again, this
time in the village hall to await being adopted into a
local family. Luckily, all four were to stay together and
live in the large house, which had spacious grounds.
They were to be blessed with a maid and chauffeur, the
like of which they had never known before.

This luxury living came to an end after a few months
when Her Ladyship fell ill and couldn't look after the
children any more. They were billeted this time in what
I can only describe as a shack. A wooden structure with
a red tin roof. Certainly downhill.

There were eight children – my four siblings and four
others – in the care of two sisters. If they misbehaved,

even in winter, they were sent outside, and if they complained of the cold, as they often did, they were told to go outside and skip. Marjorie had to be a mother to the young ones, wash and bathe them, wash the clothes and so on. Stan had had leg problems from birth and, when walking the three miles each way to school and back, he would complain that they hurt; Margie had to give him a piggyback. To keep them all going on this long walk she would line them up, one behind the other, and make them march along, singing wartime songs. Considering she was only thirteen, she did a wonderful job caring for the others.

Although the Russian convoys were no fun, I can tell you, we were blessed every six months or so with a week at home and an opportunity always to visit the children in Swanmore. It's the summer visits that I remember most clearly – they would take me up on the Downs, where we would sit, them telling me how unhappy they were and me story-telling about ice, snow, polar bears, the Northern Lights and anything to take their minds off that wooden shack and the way they lived.

Margie told of the orchard they passed on the way to school – they would collect apples which they would hide in the roadside ditch to collect on the way back to the shack. The girls would stuff them in their knickers and Stan inside his shirt, making sure they always had something to eat – as young children they were always hungry and there was never enough food to go round.

One day, again when they were en route to school,

an aircraft flew low out of the clouds, machine-gunning as it came. They threw themselves in the same roadside ditch. Often they would watch the planes in dogfights – those 'close encounters' between our planes and theirs – up in the clear blue sky. The young ones found it difficult to understand what was going on and why.

A group of evacuees from Glasgow had a happier experience. In July 1940, three 'Guiders' from Broadstairs, Kent, moved to Balendoch in Perthshire – 'right in the country, four miles from anywhere' – to run a hostel for them. The house was run on Girl Guide principles – lots of discipline, lots of teamwork – and after a short time there the matron, Esther Reiss, reported to the *Kent Girl Guide Quarterly* leaflet:

Most of the children come from the slums of Glasgow and have had no real training. They come dirty and underfed, and with practically no clothing. It is amazing to see how quickly they become part of the machinery here. Children who have had no possessions of their own are thrilled to find they have a towel, flannel, toothbrush, etc., with their own number on it, a peg for their coats, a shelf for their boots, a locker for their clothes and so on. Their baths are a source of great joy, and so are their medicines – and if one needs a dose, so does everyone. If one child has to have his temperature taken, so does everyone in that bedroom, and even if one has a dirty head, everyone else manages to have 'an awful itchy head too, miss'. Toothpaste is such a novelty that most people eat theirs – so much was eaten that we now have to keep it and put a little on everyone's brush for them.

There is a lovely big garden with woods, tennis court, kitchen garden and a wee burn, into which someone falls at least once a week. Of the war we hear nothing – no guns, no sirens, no soldiers, and only a few passing aeroplanes.

One of the other guiders kept a diary of day-to-day activities at Balendoch. These included raspberry picking, which was not only new to children from the slums, but also enabled them to earn a little pocket money:

Every morning a little army set off, in their oldest clothes, complete with cord and hook (generally known as a cleat) for the berry field. On arrival, they were provided with a large pail and a small one or a luggy. The small pail was hung on the hook, which was fastened round the waist; the big pail was carried about halfway up the drill and left there, whilst the picker and a partner went on to the end of the drill and started picking raspberries as quickly as possible into the pail slung round the waist. When full, this was emptied into the big pail. When the big pail was filled, it had to be weighed and the picker was paid at the rate of ¾d per pound.[1]

On Saturday afternoons shopping expeditions take

1. ¾d is three-quarters of an old penny (from the Latin *denarius*, hence the abbreviation d). In pre-decimalisation days, there were twelve pennies in a shilling (known colloquially as a 'bob') and twenty shillings in a pound. Sums such as three shillings and sixpence were referred to as 'three and six' and often written 3/6. In terms of purchasing power, you could buy a large loaf of bread or a quart (a bit over a litre) of milk for 9d each – about 4p; the tram fare across south London was 4d – less than 2p. But bear in mind that if you were earning £5 a week you were doing pretty well.

place and the workers are able to see the fruits of their labours – sandals, socks, gloves, banking accounts even, begin to appear at Balendoch.

In the summer of 1942, the house was locked up and the residents were taken on a camping holiday at Auchterarder:

What an exciting time we all had getting ready for this. Equipment for thirty-six campers – bedding, billies, groundsheets, tents, screening, shovels and all the other thousand and one things one needs in camp.

What a pile of stuff it was too and at last the great day dawns – in pouring rain – and a van loaned by the WVS [Women's Voluntary Service] arrives to collect that pile of stuff. After much planning and struggling it is packed and sets out on its journey. Then comes the bus to collect the human freight and convey it to the station at Coupar Angus. And the rain it is simply pouring down!

In spite of wartime restrictions, the Railway Company had reserved compartments for us and we travelled in absolute comfort from Coupar Angus to Gleneagles. From here, we walked over the fields to our campsite. The rain had stopped by now and we enjoyed the walk. When we got to the top of the hill we had to drop down into the valley, where we came on our campsite – a lovely spot by the River Ruthven – a very tiny little river, but a very exciting one. There were several little wooden bridges across it – trout to be caught, we hoped. Little waterfalls and some pools in which to swim....

At last the van arrived and up went our tents – our

beds were unpacked – the kitchen fire was lit and we had our first meal in camp – and then down came the rain once more – and for two weeks, it hardly ever stopped. But did we worry? No fear. It was a lovely fortnight and everyone is going back next year.

Nancy also introduced urban children to a new way of life. She taught at a school that was evacuated from Hayes in Middlesex to the tiny village of Twyford in Buckinghamshire:

The London children weren't used to the country, so blackberrying and going in fields and daft things like that were all completely new to them. They had no idea about blackberrying – most of them had never seen a blackberry before. We went on 1 September, just two days before war was declared, and there was a field covered in buttercups. It was nothing special to me because I'd been brought up in the country, but these children couldn't believe it – they literally didn't know what it was. They were about nine or ten, and quite excited by lots of things, but they were frightened, too – frightened in case a bull got them. We were always reassuring them that they'd be all right, but everything was so unfamiliar to them.

At first our kids only went to school part time; the village school used the building in the mornings and we went in the afternoon. So that was a bit awkward: we got the feeling that no one really wanted us. We'd been evacuated because everyone thought that the bombing was going to start straight away, but then we had six months of what they call the Phoney War, and most of the mothers fetched their children back again. After that the few that remained were integrated with the village schoolchildren and it got easier for everyone.

When we first went to Twyford I stayed with a lady who had, I think, been a maid or a cook somewhere grand. She had this new council house and she was very careful of it and very proud of it; she wasn't going to take in any children – she only wanted the teachers. So my friend and I had to go and live in this palace where you hardly dared to step anywhere because she was so house-proud. We literally had to put paper down on the floor to walk on. Her poor husband – he was ever such a nice old boy, worked on a farm, and she henpecked him something terrible. And of course he was always coming home dirty to this beautiful clean house. She fed us all right, but she wasn't very nice and you were always afraid you were going to upset her somehow.

After I couldn't endure that anymore, I went to stay with one of the local teachers, Mrs Hughes, and that was much better. She taught the infants and she had two children of her own, so she was quite human.

We were there during the Blitz, and we could just see the glow, the haze of smoke and burning over London – and that's a long way, really, forty or fifty miles. We didn't have any bombs, not even stray ones. I suppose we were too remote for anyone to bother with us – there was only a bus once a week!

You couldn't get out of Twyford except by borrowing a bike to get to the station. Calvert was the nearest, two or three miles away. You could get to London from there – slowly. The bus went to Bicester, but once a month I had to go into Buckingham to fetch our wages from the bank – mine and the other evacuee teacher's. That was about eight or nine miles, so after a certain amount of puzzling over what we should do, I found a boyfriend who took me there on his motorbike. This was much to the concern of the villagers, who didn't think it was right. They thought it was dangerous – there was no question of crash helmets in those days, you took your chance – and also it was a bit naughty, a bit 'fast'. There was a big hill, too – I was a little bit scared of that, but I didn't let on.

We used sometimes to go to the pub and play darts. Before the war that might have been seen as a bit fast, too, but the Red Lion was quite respectable. We were away from home, anyway, and Mrs Hughes suggested I go with her, so it must have been okay. I think we mostly drank lemonade, so it wasn't too debauched.

Joan wasn't evacuated as such, but she travelled back and forth between relatives' homes:

I was born in London and had lots of relations there, but by the time war broke out, we'd moved to Northamptonshire and lived in a village just outside Northampton. Before the war, my dad always insisted that we have a week's holiday at the seaside every summer.

I was a very lucky person. I had my mum and dad, but my mum's youngest sister and her husband didn't have any children of their own, so I was also their daughter, by proxy. They were in London and every holiday I begged to go back up to London and stay with them, and I was allowed to. After we'd been to Bournemouth or wherever, we'd get the train to London, drop me at my aunt's and then Mum, Dad and my sister would go on home and leave me there for a week.

We always travelled by train. We'd had a car until my sister was born – that was when I was six – but when she came along the car had to go, we couldn't afford it any more, and I wasn't very happy about that. I thought we needed a car much more than we needed a baby.

My stay in London was always towards the end of August, but in 1939 Dad was worried about all the talk of war and decided that London wasn't safe, so I had to go home with them and not have my extra week's holiday. I can remember being furious. And then a week later war was declared, so I suppose Dad had a point. My aunt's birthday was that very day – 3 September – but I don't suppose we'd have done much celebrating.

The following summer, the Battle of Britain had just started and Mum had to go into hospital for an operation. Dad worked in dispatch and transport for a company that had gone over to manufacturing aeroplane parts, so he was working all hours, seven days a week; Mum was going to be in hospital for a while, so there was nobody to look after us. We had to go back home to the family. All the aunts and uncles were working, so it was decided that the best place for us to go was to a great-aunt, my grandmother's sister, and her husband, who lived in Southall, on the outskirts of London. It seemed silly to move us so close to the bombing, but Mum and Dad really had no choice.

Anyway, this great-aunt and uncle had never had children. They were both retired, but in their working life she'd been a lady's maid and he'd been a butler. They had no idea how to look after us, and my sister, who was four by this time, ran them round her little finger. It was really funny.

We stayed with them for about six weeks. By that time Mum was out of hospital and Dad decided they could cope and we should come home. And I can remember very plainly, we were on the bus, going from Southall back to Palmer's Green, where my aunt and uncle lived. We were going to stay overnight there and Dad was coming to fetch us the next day. And we were caught up in an air raid. The bus stopped and we all had to get off and go into a shelter – which I did not like, because it was a public shelter. My great-aunt in Southall hadn't had an Anderson shelter in the garden, but the people next door did, so if there was a daylight raid we were packed off into next-door's garden with their children and told to behave ourselves and stay in. Quite often we'd be outside, though, watching the planes, because they were exciting.

Jean was another who moved from a seemingly safe place to somewhere that was likely to be more dangerous:

I was born in Melton in Suffolk, but shortly after the war started we moved to Windsor to live with my grandparents. Father was in the RAF, so whenever he had leave, he could go to Windsor and see my mother and me as well as his parents. We stayed there throughout the war.

I can remember big guns positioned at the top of the road, anti-aircraft guns. They used to go off and fire at planes coming over and I used to scream the house down. I don't actually remember that – my mother told me about it – but I do remember the fear that I felt.

At school we had to practise going down into the air-raid shelter, and practise carrying our dinner plate down with us, because whenever the siren went off, we were supposed to go down into the shelter, even if we were in the middle of our meal. But we lived just round the corner and whenever the sirens went, I just used to run home. I always seemed to have a cold, winter or summer, and my mother blamed the shelters for being cold and damp. She thought I would end up getting pneumonia and she was quite happy for me to avoid the shelter, but now I think about it, I must have played havoc with the roll call – they must always have thought I was missing. But I don't remember getting into trouble about it, so perhaps they knew what was going on and realised I was safely at home.

CHAPTER 3

'HALF A CUSTARD CREAM AND A BIT OF A GINGER NUT'

If there was an advantage to knowing that war was on its way, it was that the country had time to prepare. In addition to organising evacuation and issuing gas masks, there was rationing. For petrol, this started almost immediately; the first foods were rationed in January 1940.

The reason for this was simple: before the war, Britain imported about two-thirds of its food, and it was easy for an enemy to interfere with supplies to an island nation. Ships bringing supplies from North America and elsewhere were targeted by German U-boats as part of a deliberate policy of starving Britain out. What is known as the Battle of the Atlantic is regarded as having started the day war was declared and stopped only on VE Day, in May 1945; in the course of it, some 3,500 merchant ships were sunk. That is a lot of food and supplies, much of it bound for Britain, sent to the bottom of the ocean.

Rationing was intended both to eke out limited supplies and to distribute them fairly. Each individual was issued with a ration book containing coupons that indicated what they were entitled to. When you bought your ration of cheese or eggs or meat – and you still had to buy it; the coupons were a permit rather than a substitute for money – the shopkeeper either cut out or signed the relevant coupons to show that you had had your share. And there was no shopping around for bargains or for the chance to buy a bit extra: you signed up with a grocer's, a butcher's and so on, and that was where you did your shopping.

Ration books came in different colours. Most adults had buff ones; pregnant women, nursing mothers and children under five, who were regarded as most in need of good nutrition, had green ones, giving them first choice if fruit was available, as well as a more generous allocation of milk and eggs. Blue books were issued to children between the ages of five and sixteen, entitling them to more than the buff but less than the green contingent.

However fair rationing might have been (if everyone stuck to the rules), it didn't alter the fact that there was less food to go round. The government encouraged people to eat healthily, to keep chickens for eggs and meat, to grow their own vegetables ('digging for victory') and not to buy new clothes or furnishings when they could 'make do and mend'. In rural areas there always seems to have been an extra bit of butter to be swapped for a cauliflower or two, but in cities, queuing for hours in the hope of getting a couple of sausages became commonplace.

There were shortages of other things, too. Factories that had manufactured cars or bikes now produced military vehicles; metal that might once have made saucepans or children's toys was given over to munitions.

There was plenty of advice, in newspapers and on the radio, about diet and nutrition in times of shortage. The Ministry of Food created characters such as Potato Pete, who encouraged people to eat potatoes, which didn't have to be imported, and Doctor Carrot, offering a high vitamin A content that would help you see in the blackout. Recipes for making the most of these basics abounded. Carrot-cap salad, recommended for women who valued their good complexion, involved tossing potatoes in oil and vinegar and adding them to a salad bowl of lettuce or watercress with a few chives or rings of spring onion, then topping the whole with masses of grated carrot. Potato fingers were, to all intents and purposes, fish fingers without the fish; potato carrot pancakes were mashed potato whipped to a creamy texture with diced carrots added. The traditional Irish dish champ became the patriotic-sounding 'wartime champ' – potatoes, carrots, shredded cabbage, milk and a pat of margarine for each helping.

And so it went on. It was all good for you and good for the war effort, but it couldn't be described as exciting.

Nevertheless, the campaign had its fans. Audrey remembers:

My mother used to listen to the Radio Doctor – Dr Charles Hill. Every Monday, I think it was, he used to give some sort of recipe or advice on how to eat healthily. He had the most lovely, gentle, mellifluous voice. Years and years later, probably in the late 1970s, in Hertfordshire, we were involved in fund-raising for a local respite home, which was a large house that needed a lift. Dr Hill was by that time quite an elderly gentleman but he lived locally and he did the radio appeal for this lift. As soon as I heard his voice it took me back to childhood. My mother was devoted to him – I think she even had his picture pinned up on the wall.

Food shortages meant you had to be inventive, as Wendy remembers:

My mother worked hard and we were self-sufficient in many ways. Chickens and rabbits produced eggs and meat, and I think we made mittens from the rabbit fur. We also grew lots of fruit and vegetables. We children did the fruit picking and we all had small plots, growing radishes, carrots and weedy little flowers called stocks – all from Woolworths' seed packets bought with our pocket money.

Connie from Liverpool also recalls her mother being a great one for making the most of what she had:

She managed to make cakes out of meagre things. I had a regular job on a Sunday morning: she'd give me a big bowl with a meagre bit of butter, a bit of margarine and a drop of milk, and I'd mix it all together so that the margarine didn't taste so awful.

In fact, food shortages changed Connie's life:

When I was about sixteen, one of my cousins who lived in Southampton joined the air force and was due to go to Blackpool as a trainee RAF officer. So he was going to come to visit us for the weekend. My mother was at the shops because she'd heard that the butcher had some sausages. The word used to go around when something like that happened, and everyone would go and queue in the hope that there would be some left when they got to the front. My mother got chatting to another lady in the queue and was saying that her nephew was coming for the weekend. 'But I don't know what I'm going to do, because I haven't got a spare bed.'

'Oh, don't worry,' said this lady. 'I've got a camp bed. You can borrow it with pleasure. Where do you live?' It turned out that she lived in the same road as us and she became a great friend. Her name was Mrs Neil and she invited me to go to piano lessons with her niece and come back to her for supper afterwards, so I started to do that, once a week on a Wednesday. She had a son in the forces and after a while, probably Christmas 1944, she said, 'I wish you'd send my son a Christmas airgraph.' These were special airmail letters that you could only send to people in the services. You could get them at other times of the year, but in December they were printed with a Christmas greeting.

'I can't do that,' I said. 'I don't know him.'

'Well, he knows all about you. I've told him about you and he'd love that.'

So I wrote and in no time at all I got a reply, so we started to write to each other – and eventually I married him. It would never have happened if my mother and Mrs Neil hadn't been queuing for sausages together.

Queuing for almost everything became a way of life, as Margaret remembers:

I can remember queuing for a whole morning for a rabbit, because rabbit wasn't on coupons; and possibly queuing for two hours for a small cake. Not because you didn't want to make a cake, but because you had nothing to make a cake with.

Tony recalls changes his family made in order to feed themselves:

Before the war we had grass and one of those old push mowers, but then I remember my dad digging up all the lawn and turning it the other way up on a heap to let it rot and turning it over for potatoes and onions and carrots.

As well as growing vegetables, we also had quite a lot of chickens and they hated me. My mum was always cooking up potato skins and cabbage leaves and mixing them with meal to feed the chickens. She'd go down to their shed and let them out into a big wire run and they'd come round her, but if I went near, they'd peck me and chase me around – they just didn't like me.

We ate quite a few rabbits – they weren't on ration and I loved it. I had an uncle who was a butcher and I think we did supplement our rations with things he gave us.

Audrey in Weymouth, Dorset, aged four when war broke out, also recalls that her parents found ways and means of providing for the family:

My cousin's parents kept a grocer's shop and although things were rationed, we might have got a few 'extras' from them. We had a lot of fruit in the garden, and we bottled that. We even had loganberries, which you don't often see now – a whole pathway of loganberries, and we used to pick them in the morning and have them for breakfast with porridge. My mother kept three chickens for eggs, but for some reason they didn't lay and my father said we had to get rid of them. My mother couldn't bring herself to kill them, so the butcher came and took them away: we didn't even eat them.

We had relations who lived in the country and they used to come in by bus and bring rabbits. I remember Spam and corned beef and whale meat – I don't think I liked that. And as we lived by the sea, we had quite a lot of fish. A man used to come round with his cart, with mackerel that he'd just caught. Everybody would go out with their enamel plates and buy two or three mackerel. Soused mackerel, my mother used to cook – with vinegar; she'd just pop it in the oven, perhaps with some peppercorns.

The milkman used to come round with a churn – we'd leave a jug outside the kitchen door for him to fill. We were very friendly with him and if my mother put a saucer out as well, he would put some milk in that for the dog.

Billy's family also made the most of what was available:

On a Sunday we had mince and tatties or stew, which would have had beef in it but I remember that it had pork sausages too. I always enjoyed that.

We grew our own vegetables – the normal British vegetables like potatoes, carrots, turnips, cabbages, cauliflower, leeks and spring onions. So we were able to grow food for ourselves, to give us soup: during the week soup was the order of the day. I don't remember us ever going without bread material, because my job in the morning, before I went to school, was to run to the bakery and get half a dozen rolls. Rolls were a staple diet in the morning – I would have two with butter, until the butter ran out. I hated margarine, I never touched the stuff. But things did run out. I remember my father, who was a miner, saying that towards the end of the war he went for six months on grapefruit marmalade on his 'piece' – the lunch that he took with him down the pit. There was nothing else that he could put on his rolls. But I don't remember ever being hungry in the sense that we saw on the newsreels of what was happening to people in other parts of Europe. Obviously, my father, being in a heavy industry, had to be fed – you couldn't go weak down the pit – but it was as much home-grown as we could manage.

There was jam, because we could go out into the wilderness in this area and pick blackberries for free. Of course the problem was the sugar, so my mother saved up several weeks' worth of rations to get enough to make the jam. One of the things that happened was that we had less sugary tea – people gave up taking sugar in tea in order to use their ration for things like making jam. There was a whole host of things which, in a more ample time, you wouldn't have needed to think about.

June in Andover recognised the advantages of being in a market town surrounded by prosperous countryside:

You could get a boiling fowl and, if you didn't mind having to boil it up before you roasted it, it could turn out quite nicely. But you weren't buying things in plastic boxes – you invariably had to pluck the chicken first. There was no shortage of rabbits or hares. At the start of the war there used to be game birds like grouse – they were off the ration – but later there wasn't so much of that because they weren't reared the way they used to be. The gamekeepers were all taken off and put in the infantry or whatever, so that petered out a bit. But you could nearly always find a rabbit somewhere.

Domestic Science lessons were a way of getting a bit extra. June continues:

The headmistress put in for lots of rations because we were learning to cook. She had an allocation of meat and cheese, margarine, flour and sugar, so if we got extra, we got more food at the end of the day. If we were making summer pudding, say, we'd be asked to bring along something like rhubarb, because we all had that in the garden. But the Ministry of Food seemed quite satisfied that we were entitled to extras because we were learning to cook.

Sylvia, leaving school at sixteen in 1943, was taken on as a trainee nurse at a small children's hospital on the edge of Luton:

There were only about eighty children, who had been evacuated from Swanley in Kent, to a country house which had been converted into a hospital. Having been a country house, it had very big wooden shutters, which were ideal for blackouts, but most of the children had orthopaedic tuberculosis – a form of TB that affects the bones – and the hospital was very keen on fresh air. So when you were on night duty, you had to throw the shutters and windows open for an hour, which meant creeping around without any lights on.

We did quite well, us nurses. The hospital had inherited some of the staff of the house, including the cook and her husband, who was the gamekeeper. She was a marvellous cook and we seemed to get extremely good food. I think probably she knew everybody in the district and wasn't above a bit of bartering. She certainly made the best custard tarts I have ever tasted. We didn't keep cows, but there were plenty in the fields round about, so there was no shortage of milk. She must have had access to hens, too, because she couldn't have made these custard tarts with powdered egg, which was horrible. Very useful at the time, but not very nice. You could make a version of scrambled eggs with it, but it was very much 'a version of…'

Mushrooms used to grow in the fields, too, and if we chose to get up early in the morning and go and pick them, she would cook them for breakfast.

Vere Hodgson, keeping a diary in London, recorded, amid the shortages, the occasional treat:

Thursday 13th August, 1942: Had some plums tonight – raw. What a treat. I asked the Old Pole [the local greengrocer] humbly for a pound from a green-looking lot. But he slipped to the back and produced a superior sort of basket and said: 'Two pounds.' I demurred. At this he regarded me severely and remarked: 'When I tell you to have two pounds, you'd better have two pounds.' Wonderful – five pence a pound. Have been eating them tonight.

The following summer, she spent a week at the home of a friend in Chipping Campden in Gloucestershire:

Thursday 8th July, 1943: We could get fruit! Campden is full of cherry orchards. As we came along, we gazed anxiously at the trees, hoping there were cherries left for us. There was no holding us back, so fruit-starved are we. After tea we went and bought some from an old chap straight off the tree. One and sixpence a pound – but he gave us good weight. In any case there is nothing else to buy here, not even picture postcards. Bernard said I should be ill, but far from it – my system just absorbed redcurrants, strawberries and plums…what a feast!

Anne remembers her mother and aunt having a treat of a different kind:

One summer my mother got hold of some elderflowers and made elderflower champagne. Goodness knows why, because she and Aunt Ida, who lived with us, were strict teetotallers. It was a hot summer and she put it in the pantry under the stairs, but she must have done something wrong because the bottles exploded. So she tried again the next year and I remember her sitting in the garden with my aunt and saying how refreshing this was and let's have another. By the end they must both have been quite tipsy. She was telling someone the next day that she felt a bit shaky and they said, 'You must have been a little drunk.' But oh no, she said, she belonged to the Band of Hope – she'd signed the pledge and never drank anything. She had no idea that something that was just sugar, water and flowers could possibly be alcoholic.

For children, treats normally came in the form of sweets. Tony recalls one source of these:

One friend's father was always going off somewhere – I don't know what he did, but whenever he came back, he would bring exciting things. The one I remember is a stick of rock, which he shared out between us kids. We probably got about an inch each, but it was a real luxury.

Albert's father also had a useful friend:

My father worked on the railway; he was one of the senior clerks in Whitehaven Bransty station, dealing with lots of people who were using the railway to send parcels all over the country. He got to know a little old lady who had a sweet shop. Miss Rooke was her name. Her shop was like something from Dickens: lots of empty jars and empty tins. She had her storeroom at the back and when my brother and I went into the sweetshop with Dad, which we did sometimes during the holidays, she was a bent little old lady in dark brown clothes – she was Dickensian too – and she would greet Dad with a little wave. Then she would sneak through into the back of the shop and come back with a couple of little bags of something: sweets over and above what we were allowed on the ration, which was lovely.

Anne's aunt was another source of 'extras':

She worked for Lovell's, the local sweet and chocolate factory – Toffee Rex, they used to make there. Occasionally if they'd had to stop production because of an air-raid warning, Toffee Rex would turn into fudge, which wasn't what it was supposed to be. So when Ida came home she'd sometimes have a bag of things that had gone wrong, which was absolutely tremendous. I remember this 'what should have been toffee that was fudge' very clearly – oh, we loved it.

Maggie had one treat from an unexpected source:

Mother put a notice down near Barry Docks offering bed and breakfast and we often used to get ships' captains coming and staying the night. They'd brought in fruit and veg and things like that and I suppose they were having a night ashore while the cargo was unloaded. One of these captains was the first black man I had ever seen – he was very, very nice and I remember that he gave me a banana. I'd eaten an orange before, so I knew how to peel an orange and I stuck my fingers into the sides of the banana in the same way.

'No, no, no,' the gentleman said, and showed me how

to strip the peel down from the top. I remember being uncertain about it: I wasn't sure if I liked it or not.

We were in Wales during the war because that's where my mother came from, but my father's parents lived in Tilehurst, just outside Reading in Berkshire. How we got there I don't know, but we did go to visit sometimes. Granddad kept rabbits. He and Grandma had a long garden and there were hutches right along one side of it. Granddad would breed them, kill them and sell them to the butcher's, so he had a very good little number going there.

And he had what he called a banana tree at the bottom of the garden. We're talking about a time when I was perhaps four or five. Any time we visited he used to say, 'Well, it's a good job you've come today, because I'm sure there's a banana left. I've picked all the others, but I think there's one left.'

So we'd go down the garden and sure enough, there would be one banana on the tree – because he'd tied it on. And of course I knew how to eat it, because that gentleman who stayed with us in Barry had shown me. I have no idea how Granddad got those bananas. He was an artful old devil – very nice, but an artful old devil. As I said, he had a very good little business with his rabbits and he doubtless knew someone who could help him out with bananas when I was coming to visit.

Granddad's artfulness could sometimes backfire on him, though. Maggie continues:

These grandparents came to visit us in Barry one summer. I was finicky about my food – it was very difficult to get me to eat anything I didn't like. We couldn't afford to waste food, of course, but I didn't care about that. Mother became a dab hand at scraping my leftovers on to another plate and serving it up in a different guise at the next meal.

But on this occasion I can remember sitting up at the table and Mother saying, 'Come on, Margaret, get on with your...' whatever it was and me moaning and saying I didn't want to. Granddad was sitting next to me and he'd finished his lunch, so he said to me, 'I tell you what. I'm going to prove to you that, if you eat all your food, the fairies will leave some money under your plate.'

I looked at him, and he sat up straight and waved his hands over his plate as if he were casting a spell, and he said, 'Fairy, fairy, I have eaten all my lunch. Please leave some money under my plate.' He lifted the plate up and there was a two-shilling piece.

'Oh!!!' I gasped and of course I gobbled my food after that. Just as I had finished, he said, 'What's that over there?' and pointed out the window. So I looked and couldn't see anything and he said, 'It's gone now. So let's see what's been left under your plate.'

So I did the same spell – 'Fairy, fairy, I have eaten all my lunch' and so on – and lifted up the plate. There was a ten-shilling note! Ten shillings was a lot of money: half a week's wages for some people. Of course, Granddad had slipped it out of his pocket and slid it under my plate while I was looking out the window. I like money now and I loved money then, so I grabbed it and put it in my pocket. Then Granddad said, 'Tell you what, I'll look after it for you.' But I said, 'No, I can look after it,' and he never did get that ten shillings back. I was told years later that he said to Mother and Father, 'You owe me ten bob [shillings]' and Father said, 'Well, you silly bugger, you shouldn't have put it there.'

I ate up my meals with a lot more enthusiasm after then, but of course Mother always had to put something under my plate to keep me doing it. It was only ever threepence or sixpence, though – Granddad's extravagance was never repeated.

Bananas were such a rarity that they caused trouble in Anne's household:

There was one time when I went with my mother to the Co-op, which was the grocery she was registered with. The woman in front of us in the queue that day was Mrs Edwards, the town clerk's wife. The grocer said to her, 'Oh, Mrs Edwards, these are in today' and handed her a brown paper bag. It didn't mean anything to me, but Mum said, 'Those are bananas', so when we got to the front of the queue, she asked for some and was told there weren't any. She was furious, because any bananas that came in were meant for the children and Mrs Edwards didn't have any children.

'I'll have my ration book, then, please,' she said, 'and I'll take it elsewhere.'

And she did. She went to the grocer in the market. She didn't do any better than anyone else there, but it was the principle of the thing and this new grocer did have tins of broken biscuits at the back of his stall. They had a glass cover on them and he would lift up the cover, put in one of those big scoops and scoop the biscuits into a paper bag. You didn't have to pay coupons for those, so we could have a bag of broken biscuits. There might be half a custard cream and a bit of a ginger nut – that was a real treat.

In addition to food being in short supply, Shirley's recollections are of school meals, in particular, being horrible:

The thing I hated most was chocolate pudding, and I love chocolate. I'm sure there was no chocolate in this: they must have coloured it brown with something else. At school they quite sensibly converted the basement into the dining room – we used to call it the dungeons, and it served as our shelter. So that if a raid came when we were having lunch, we didn't have to abandon our food and clatter downstairs.

Charlotte was at school in Speyside and had a happier experience:

It was the prep school for Gordonstoun, a wonderful,

wonderful place. We ate very well – there was no privation, really. Certain things, obviously, were rationed, but there were local farms and the school was very, very well managed by the headmaster's wife so we didn't go without. We had a form of muesli which was absolutely delicious. The school had European connections, so somebody had probably imported the recipe: muesli was a Swiss invention that was hardly known in Britain then. Ours had little bits of crisp apple in it, green apple with the peel still on.

They had a way of poaching eggs that was delicious, too. We had dried egg back at home – it was rather nice in its way, it just wasn't like egg. But at school we had more eggs than just the one a week that was the ration: the headmaster's wife must have kept chickens along with everything else she did. We did really, really well. I remember a choice between Spam and corned beef, which may not sound much, but was a lot more than a lot of people had.

Sylvia, twelve when war broke out, fantasised about things she had never had:

At home, news time was absolutely sacrosanct: whenever there was a news bulletin, the radio had to go on and we listened in silence. And we listened to the radio all the time. Before the war we'd often listened to Radio Luxembourg, particularly on a Sunday, when the BBC was very serious but Luxembourg had music and variety shows. I don't really remember the programmes, but I do remember the advertising: 'We are the Ovaltineys' and ads for Horlicks, too. Radio Luxembourg closed down during the war, but it coloured the stories I used to tell to my younger sister, with whom I shared a bed. My older sister had always told me bedtime stories, and now I made up stories to tell to my younger one. In one of them every now and then, at a pause in their adventures, everyone sat down and drank Horlicks. I had never tasted it; it would have been a great luxury, so I obviously thought it was exciting enough to put into a story. Because of the advertisements we really wanted to be able to drink Horlicks and Ovaltine, but we only got as far as cocoa.

Sylvia's diet grew fractionally more exciting when she arrived in Luton, a much larger place than she was used to:

Of course, nobody in the village had coffee. I don't think I'd ever heard of coffee until I was sixteen and went nursing. I seem to remember then that we could have a cup of coffee and a doughnut in a cafe for sixpence – but we could only do it at the beginning of the month, when we'd just been paid. We got all our keep, and our uniforms, but we didn't have much money.

We also had three jam jars with our names on the outside, and on Mondays, into each one you had to put your week's ration of sugar and a lump of butter and a lump of margarine. Now I come to think of it, it must have got very nasty by the end of the week in the summer, because we used to carry the jars around with us rather than leaving them in the cool of the larder – otherwise, what would we have done if we went for a meal that required sugar or butter?

I remember one small child being admitted to the hospital and saying, 'My mummy says to tell you that I only eat the *best* margarine.' You could buy something called 'special margarine', which was more expensive than the only other brand available, but I can't imagine that the hospital splashed out on it for that little girl.

During this time in Luton, Sylvia had one memorable break from the monotony of the wartime diet:

My father had been posted to the Azores by this time. One morning, on my day off, I was asleep in bed and a porter came up, knocked and came in with an enormous wooden crate addressed to me. He left it and went away to get some tools to take the lid off. It was full of, at the top, a layer of bananas; under that, a layer of oranges and below that, pineapples. It had come from my father. Somehow – and it must have been totally illegally – he'd got it flown over to his RAF base in Scotland and from there put on the railway to come to me in Luton. And when I say it was enormous, it must have been, because it seems to me that we were all – all the staff and the children – able to have a banana. Looking back, I think that that can't be true; there can't have been that many bananas, but we certainly all had a piece of fruit. The small children in the hospital had never seen exotic fruit like that. One little girl said to me, 'Isn't there a war on where your daddy is?' And afterwards we almost all had very sore mouths; we just weren't used to the acid in the oranges and pineapples.

I also remember a group of friends and me walking down the hill into Luton, and you know how you eat a banana, with the peel pulled back? We were passed by a convoy of soldiers, all whistling and shouting at this group of girls walking along, eating bananas. We must have been quite a sight.

When it came to celebrations, even more ingenuity than usual was called for. Bridget remembers an occasion when she was seven:

My brother was born at the end of 1941 and was christened the next summer in the City of London. Our father was churchwarden at St Lawrence Jewry, but we couldn't have the christening there because it had been blown to smithereens the previous Christmas, the night that that famous photo of St Paul's standing amid the flames was taken. So Martin was christened at St Mary Woolnoth instead. The vicar had to take a silver butter dish to put the holy water in, and he gave it to my brother, who still has it. But he's in the register at St Lawrence Jewry, as having been christened there. All the bomb damage was still smoking – it wasn't in flames, but you were still aware of it. It was weird.

Then we had a christening tea at the Great Eastern Hotel and nobody believed me for years when I told this story, but when the christening cake came in, it was completely fake. There was a whole cardboard frame that looked like icing and, when you took it off, there was a tiny little cake inside. Years later, I saw a film where someone was getting married during the war; the same thing happened with their wedding cake and I said, 'There, I knew I was right!'

On a more domestic level, my brother was five years younger than me and he was allowed orange juice, which my mother sometimes made into orange jelly. She made very nice apple fritters, too. My brother also, for some reason, got a tea ration – so we were lucky, because some people were desperate for tea.

For most children, of course, birthdays were the time when celebrations mattered. Brenda in Enham, Hampshire, recalls one special cake:

My birthday is 3 August and I certainly used to have birthday parties. At some point during the war, Mum gave a home to two lads from Southampton; one didn't stay long, because he joined the forces, but the other was a bit younger and he stayed on. One time he went to see his parents in Southampton and he brought back some silver cashews, as they called them – little edible silver balls that you could decorate cakes with. His mother must have had some, I suppose, and he must have told her that my birthday was coming up – it's stayed in my mind because we didn't see them often and, that year, Mum was able to decorate my birthday cake in a way that made it special.

Pauline in Luton also has an August birthday and remembers being given a bicycle:

It was my first two-wheeler. We had to go to Dunstable on the bus to collect it, and then we had to walk all the way back because we couldn't take it on the bus and I didn't know how to ride it. It was a long hot walk, four or five miles.

The bike was second-hand, but in very good condition. Somebody had obviously taken care of it, and although I can only have been about five or six, I looked after it as if it were a real treasure. You did in those days. Not only were you taught to look after your things, but you knew that if anything went wrong with it, you wouldn't be getting another.

Joyce in Suffolk also remembers her first bike, another summer birthday present:

My grandmother used to spoil me, I think because I was the eldest, and I remember her giving me a little bike when I was about six and teaching me to ride. She never wanted to let go of the back, so she used to run up the road, holding on. She managed quite well, because she was quite young, really, for a grandmother: she wasn't that old when my father was born and he wasn't that old when I was born. So she was able to keep running along with me until I got my balance.

Sue and her sisters didn't have birthday parties as such...

... but we did sort of celebrate them – perhaps a couple of friends from the village but, remember, it wasn't easy for people to get around and we were up the hill and not exactly easy to reach. But I still have the 'baby's log book' that my mother kept about me and she recorded my third birthday, 31 July 1943. My sister Margaret had turned four a few months before:

[Susie] has loved every minute of it from cards at breakfast and parcels after to her tea party in the afternoon. I got her a second-hand tricycle from Tom [my father, serving in India] and me and it is highly successful. Margaret commandeered it at first, but Susie very soon got the idea of pedalling, tho' is not quite as safe as Margaret yet! The other two both enjoyed themselves too, tho' Margaret had to be occasionally reassured. She couldn't quite remember that she'd had all the fuss on her birthday.

There's a photo of me sitting proudly on this tricycle with a basket hanging from the handlebars. In my imagination I'm obviously imitating Mum by cycling off to do the shopping. My mother used to cycle everywhere, with a sort of basket on the back that she would carry one of us in. She must have struggled to cycle up those hills with a child on the back of the bike.

Particularly when fathers were absent, it was often a case of 'little things mean a lot'. Evelyn in Kendal wrote to her husband about their daughter's sixth birthday:

Thursday – and Jeanne's birthday! A glorious sunshiny day, and beautiful roses to greet her! I handed her paints, and sent through the post the handkerchiefs you suggested. Jeanne was so happy and said, 'Dear, dear daddy. He always thinks about me.' In the case I enclosed a note as from you. 'Just a little keepsake on my darling's sixth birthday – Daddy.' No, dear! they will never forget their daddy. Already the memory is too deeply impressed upon their minds, and you're just a hero to them.

One of Maggie's first presents was a teddy bear:

His name was Peter. I loved him and still love him – I still have him. I must have been given him for my second birthday, just before the war started. But I made the great mistake of thinking that his hair was growing too long, so I cut it and was dismayed to find that it never grew back. I've had a bald teddy bear for eighty years, more or less.

It wasn't just food and toys that were in short supply. Clothing factories turned to producing parachutes and uniforms, so again civilians had to do their best with what they had. Clothing rationing was introduced on 1 June 1941 and a few days later Rose in Bromley wrote to her sister in Switzerland:

What do you think of our clothes rationing? I think it is the funniest thing ever. Tickles me to death, especially using margarine coupons for it. For the first week, the shops did not seem to do much business, no one knowing quite where they were, I think, but things are getting more normal now.

I have now made a bits and pieces petti[coat] of odd lengths or satin and a bit of lace I had left over from your set. It doesn't look at all bad. Mum did some featherstitching up the front. I am now going to make another one with more oddments. This will save a few coupons! I shall make another woolly jumper, too, I think; there is plenty of bits of wool left over. Must think out a pattern. Lil is trying to finish off the undie set she started about three years ago. It comes out periodically.

Bridget remembers that reusing bits and pieces became a way of life:

It annoys me so much when they talk nowadays about the royals 'recycling' clothes – it means they've worn the same dress twice. Recycling for us meant when you took the sleeves out of one thing and stuck it in the bodice of something else. My brother had a dear little siren suit, like the one Churchill used to wear, made out of Mummy's camel-hair coat. I think there was a dressmaker down the road who did that, but Mummy did make some of our clothes. I have a photo of me in a knitted dress she made, with a plain blue body – royal blue – and stripy sleeves in red, yellow and green; on the skirt there are patch pockets in a different material. The photo is in black and white, of course, but I remember the dress vividly. It's a priceless photo because, in it, Mummy is wearing a scarf wound into a turban, a bit like the kind Mrs Churchill wore, making them look like the women in the factories, showing solidarity. And we're standing in the garden, with the brick shelter behind. It's a perfect picture of life during the war.

Interestingly, in the same album, there's a photo of all the family at my baby cousin's christening in 1941 and everyone's looking very smart: they haven't given up the struggle! They still had frocks and suits that hadn't worn out. But of course it got worse as the war dragged on – the shortages got worse and you had to make do and mend all the more.

Shirley, at secondary school by the end of the war, recalls being struck by the contrast between the drab teachers and a new member of staff:

We knew every garment that our teachers wore – they got more and more threadbare as the war wore on. But towards the end of the war we had a new French teacher, who wore orange lipstick and orange rouge. She curled her ginger hair and she had smart clothes, in a wide variety of colours, which she made herself. We thought she was terrific.

Margaret has memories of both frugality and extravagance:

I remember undoing a sweater that I'd knitted – I might have grown out of it, or perhaps it had shrunk in the wash. But then I washed the wool and knitted it up into something else. Everyone did that sort of thing. Not because you couldn't afford something else, but because if you didn't have the coupons, you couldn't have it.

I had very narrow feet – double A – and I bought a pair of shoes from Russell & Bromley. They were beautiful and they cost five pounds. When I came home I burst into tears, because that was a month's salary. But they were the nicest shoes I've ever had.

Brenda, living in Enham, Hampshire, also remembers frugality:

Mum worked in a factory in the village, mending parachutes. Unfortunately, she didn't get spare bits of silk to bring home – I know you could buy parachute silk and people used to make clothes from it, but we didn't get any perks like that. Mum made some of our things – she knitted a lot – but we just made do with less. You had a best pair of shoes for Sunday, to wear to church; another pair of shoes for school and then a pair of plimsolls or something for playing. And really it was the same with clothes – we didn't wear uniform at primary school, but we'd have a gym slip or something like that for school, a Sunday dress and not much more.

June's experience was similar:

As far as clothes were concerned, we had to do the best we could, with twenty coupons having to last a year and a pair of shoes needing five coupons. They gave extra coupons to older schoolchildren, provided they exceeded a certain height or weight, or if the size of the foot was closer to an adult's. Well, I didn't stand a chance with the first two – I've always been little – but I was determined to get the last one. We had to stand up in school and the teacher marked our height on the wall. She had scales to check our weight, and for the feet she marked a line a certain distance from the skirting: if our toes came over that line, she put us down as entitled to extra coupons for shoes, because it proved we were growing out of what we had. So I managed to get my foot over the line – you don't know how hard I was trying – and I got five more coupons.

School uniform was more or less abandoned in the end – nobody could afford to have a spare set of clothes. You just had to make do with what you'd got. I was an only child, so there were no big sisters to hand things down to me: I had to rely on elderly aunts. We used to go round and see if they had any leftover frocks or skirts; they might turn them over to you and say, 'Well, you can have this for what you can make out of it.' One great-aunt of mine died and when they turned out her attic, they found boxes full of old clothes and I got quite a few of these. They had to be remade, of course, but I think I got a nice pinafore dress, a skirt and a coat. We knew a lady who had a little sewing business and she did some of the work; some of the others I actually made myself.

We had sewing lessons at school and an allocation of material. I'd have been about thirteen at this time. The sewing mistress managed to persuade the headmistress that it was a bit silly for us to be making things for small children. Most of us had siblings who were quite close to us in age, so baby clothes were no good to them. The sewing mistress thought it would be better if we made something for ourselves. So we did. But it all had to be done properly – yes, we got new clothes out of it, but we had to do the seams a certain way, because it was still a sewing lesson.

For Sylvia, whose father's RAF postings kept them constantly on the move and who attended no fewer than nine different schools, uniform was only one aspect of 'fitting in':

I do know that at one stage, with all the changing schools that I did, one school I went to had brown gym slips and the next one had navy blue, but I had to keep wearing the brown one. There wasn't the money or the coupons to get me a new one. So of course I stood out and I remember that very clearly – that was something of which I did not approve. It was bad enough being a stranger, as I so often was, and on this occasion I was the only English girl in a Scottish school, so this made it even worse. But that wasn't about fashion, it was about fitting in. They used to delight in trying to make me say things like Auchtermuchty, which it took me a long time to master.

I did have some underwear made from parachute silk. I don't remember where the silk came from – perhaps my father got it from somewhere. But just as they hadn't invented teenagers at that time, I don't think we had taste in clothes. For girls living in the country, fashion was very far away. Being the middle child, I had to wear my sister's hand-me-downs, but I suppose because things weren't there, children wouldn't really have thought about what they were missing.

Jenny in Oswestry, Shropshire, fared better:

Shortly after I was born, the RAF sent my father to Canada; they were training young men to be pilots out there. He was stationed near Winnipeg and he made friends with a lovely Canadian family who used to send parcels to us via him – clothes and material in particular, I remember. My grandmother was a professional dressmaker, so I did quite well with pretty little dresses with smocking. We were lucky in that respect.

I remember one dress that I was really fond of – it had a floral pattern and I think it was made of linen, so quite good stuff. When I grew out of it, my grandmother put extra panels of plain blue material in it and eked it out so that I could keep wearing it. I have a photograph that a friend who was born the day before me sent me: it's of her birthday party, we must be four or five, and there are she and I side by side in almost identical cotton smock dresses and my baby brother in a little romper suit with a smock top, all of which my grandmother must have made.

Anne remembers that her mother was particularly clever at making clothes:

She made use of anything she could cut down. She made blankets into skirts and one of my summer dresses had been a tablecloth, a gingham one, red and white checks. It was very pretty – I felt really good in it. But there was one that was even more smart than that: she got some flour sacks, they were calico or something like that; she bleached them, then boiled them to within an inch of their lives and left them out in the sun on the hedge to dry. My aunt was getting married, so that was a big occasion and my mother made a lovely soft cream dress for me out of these flour sacks.

And that wasn't all. In those days, milk bottles had

cardboard tops with a little circle in the middle that you popped through with your thumb, so you were left with a biggish circle of cardboard with a small open circle in the middle that you could put a straw through. Well, Mother had saved up these cardboard circles and she washed them and bound embroidery silk round them with blanket stitch to make daisy shapes with pretty edging. She made thirty or so of these and stitched them individually on to the dress.

So off we went to my aunt's wedding: Mother wore her own wedding dress. My aunt, the bride, had borrowed a wedding dress from a bank of dresses that the queen had set up – if I remember rightly, the queen had asked anyone who had a wedding dress at home, from before the war, to register it so that wartime brides could borrow it for the day and have something suitable to wear. My uncle was home on leave, so he got married in his uniform and I wore this little dress made of flour sacks with beautiful bottle tops all over it. I must have been about four and it made such an impression on me. I don't remember wearing that dress any other time, which is probably just as well, because if I'd got it dirty, my mother would have had to take all the bottle tops off it before she could wash it: she couldn't really have washed the cardboard.

I had another aunt who lived with us. She was always going to dances and if I was in bed before she went out, she'd come and say goodnight to me. I'd know when she was coming up the stairs because she had a grosgrain skirt and it rustled. She had an artificial flower that she put in her hair – oh, I thought she was terribly glamorous.

Not everyone was as gifted as Anne's mother. Charlotte remembers:

My mother was hopeless at making clothes. Her mother was brilliant, but it missed out in my mother and me: I was once ticked off in a needlework exam for sighing, because I couldn't get it right. Various friends would show my mother how to cut things out on the kitchen table, but even so she would get the material the wrong way round and so on. She got clothes through a magazine called *Nursery World*. I can remember some jerseys with lovely little collars – it was a very intelligent system, people passing on clothes that their children had grown out of. School uniform was supplied, but again some of it was second-hand, handed down from older pupils. The girls at the Gordonstoun school had divided skirts – not just a boring skirt, but not trousers either. They were very, very nice.

Nice things were hard to come by, as Connie recalls, rather crossly:

I remember our next-door neighbour asking my sister if she would mind being a model for a dress she was making for her niece, who was roughly the same shape and size. Blanche was happy to oblige. Then, on the day of a summer dance that Blanche was hoping to attend, the neighbour brought the dress around for her. It had been a secret, but the dress had been for her all along. I remember being jealous and my mother telling me it would be my turn in a few years. My turn never came!

Shirley's father also had responsibility for other people's clothes:

In addition to being in the Home Guard and having to man his gun at night, he was a dry cleaner and owned a number of shops in South London, as well as the factories where the actual dry cleaning was done. A lot of Dad's business came from cleaning forces' uniforms, because people at that time generally didn't take their clothes in to be cleaned unless they were absolutely filthy – it was a bit of a luxury. But of course you couldn't wear the same pair of trousers for five years without having it cleaned. My father's shops all had big front windows that would break if a bomb was dropped in the vicinity, and then – and I hate telling you this – looters would steal the clothes. Dad had insurance and it would pay money; I'm sure it was a very small amount, but even so if you had lost your overcoat and had some money in compensation, you couldn't get another one if you didn't have the coupons. So, as far as Dad was concerned, getting the windows mended after a raid was always urgent.

One of his crew on the ack-ack [anti-aircraft] gun was

a carpenter called Harry. One day Harry was mending a church altar which had been damaged in a raid and my father came storming down the aisle and said, 'I need you immediately.' One of his shops had had its windows broken and needed to be fixed *now*. Harry protested that he had to finish the job he was doing and my father said, 'Jesus Christ is dead and he doesn't need an overcoat! Come with me.'

CHAPTER 4

'TOO MANY UNPLEASANT EXPERIENCES TO MENTION – AND BEST FORGOTTEN ANYWAY'

It may have seemed like a 'Phoney War' in Britain, but on the Continent it was real enough. By May 1940, Neville Chamberlain had resigned as prime minister and Winston Churchill had become leader of a National Government formed from all political parties. Germany had conquered Holland and Belgium; France was on the brink of collapse and fears that Hitler would invade Britain were increasing by the day. It seemed as if the German forces were sweeping through Europe and that the war was all but over.

The British Expeditionary Force – the British Army in Europe – along with a substantial number of French and Belgian troops had retreated to the vicinity of Dunkirk (Dunkerque in French), a port in the northeast of France, close to the Belgian border. Cornered and apparently helpless, they were rescued from Dunkirk's beaches with the help of an ad hoc fleet of about 850 merchant marine ships, pleasure craft, fishing boats and other privately owned vessels that sailed across the Channel to aid in the evacuation. By 4 June over 300,000 men had escaped, thanks to 'the little ships of Dunkirk', but they were exhausted from weeks of hard fighting and had had to leave behind tanks, equipment and personal possessions. The massive saving of life was hailed a triumph but, as Churchill put it, 'wars are not won by evacuations'.

John, aged six at the time, was living in Weymouth:

The first recollection I have of summer during the war is that I used to sleep under the stairs. We had the usual Anderson shelter in the garden and a Morrison shelter indoors, but I slept under the stairs. I came out one morning and was asked to be especially quiet. Under a chair in the kitchen there were two helmets with a metal ridge over the top, which I recognised as the sort of helmets that our French allies wore. I was told that there were two French soldiers resting upstairs. This was just before Dunkirk and they had been sent over to have forty-eight hours respite. Basically, all they did for those two days was sleep, eat and sleep again.

At the end of forty-eight hours, they had to go back to France, just when everyone else was on the point of being evacuated. The poor bloody French were the rearguard; they had to put themselves between the Germans and the British forces, so that we could get off.

I can see them now, these two poor men, carrying their rifles and with their steel helmets on the back of their packs. They asked us to come and wave them off, so we did. It was a beautiful sunny day. There had been perhaps two or three hundred men – a whole ship – billeted in the town for that short time, then off they had to go. Our two probably didn't survive; we certainly never heard from them again.

Jack was a member of the North Midland Corps Signals, ordered to Le Havre that spring:

My only recollection of arriving in France is of trooping down the gangplank on to the quayside and being given a tin of Maconachie's stew; as there were no facilities for heating food, the stew was eaten cold…at 6.30 a.m. As far as I can recall, we entrained for a village near Arras and, after a week or two, moved to Béthune. The Germans started their offences on the Low Countries on May 10th and from then on, in military parlance, the situation became 'fluid'. We moved at a moment's notice to the area of the break-through near the Belgian border, but in the Signals office we were issuing orders to troops which were bypassed by events, and by 25th May we received orders to make the coast in any way we could; after a couple of nightmarish days we reached the canal separating us from Bray-Dunes at De Panne.

Before crossing the canal by one of the few remaining bridges, we drove our vehicles into a field and immobilised them, burning any documents still left which might have been of use to the enemy. From Monday, 27th May, we were on the dunes, waiting to be taken off by the 'Little Ships' who had so valiantly sailed from England to rescue us. One of the great advantages of being in soft sand was that only a fairly direct hit from bombs and shells would cause fatalities…minor wounds were treatable with the few field-dressings still available. There was no food after we had finished our tinned emergency rations, and water was scarce.

Over the next few days we formed orderly queues on the beach, sometimes standing up to our knees in the sea, waiting for small boats to pick us up and take us out to larger vessels standing off-shore. I remember standing there at dusk and watching the bright phosphorescence in the gentle lapping of the tide; I wondered if the German night-bombers could see it and thus pinpoint our positions. By Friday the 31st May most of my unit had managed to get away and I was left with about twenty men. I was instructed just after mid-day to march the party to Dunkerque; it was about five miles walking on very soft sand and, in our weakened state, very tiring in heavy boots. All of us had left any personal belongings behind and just marched with rifles…the last thing a soldier parts with, if ever. We were bombed and shelled on the way, but eventually reached the mole at Dunkerque (what there was left of it) about eight or nine o'clock that night. A destroyer eventually tied up (HMS *Whitehall*, I think) with much of its superstructure and some of its armament shot away. Again, I am rather hazy about it, but I think we pulled away from the mole just after 11 p.m.

By this time there were a few hundred of us waiting to embark: infantry, signals, engineers and artillery, and we were packed on board like sardines, but the Navy, as always, was calm and matter-of-fact in the face of the greatest danger; my most vivid memory is of being given a hunk of freshly baked bread from the galley, and looking back as we sailed into the Channel to get my last sight of the burning oil-tanks of Dunkerque before I fell into an exhausted sleep.

We arrived at Dover, relieved to be home, yet ashamed to have left so much valuable equipment in France and Belgium. We looked a mess...haggard, bearded and scruffy, but, to our surprise, we were given a welcome suitable for a victorious army! The W.V.S. were there on the railway platforms at Dover with tea, sandwiches and buns, and we were put onto trains for 'an unknown destination'. We left Dover about 2 a.m. on Saturday, June 1st, 1940. So many things had happened in the three weeks since May 10th, too many unpleasant experiences to mention – and best forgotten anyway...

We finished up sometime on Saturday in Ludlow, Shropshire, and were taken to the Castle; we were not allowed to 'phone home, but were allowed to send postcards postage-free. As can be imagined, we were survivors from all sorts of regiments and our arrival had to be advised to the various H.Qs and Records Offices. I was eventually given forty-eight hours' leave and discovered that I had been posted 'Missing'.

Audrey, another small child in Weymouth, confirms the 'heroes' welcome':

It must have been a Saturday or a Sunday, because on those days my parents and I used to go for a walk in the evenings. As we walked along the street we saw soldiers coming along, and people coming out of their houses with cigarettes and biscuits and cups of tea. I was conscious of the fact that their uniforms looked a bit odd; they had obviously waded through the water to get to the little boats off the beaches at Dunkirk, because their uniforms were caked.

Somebody said that they were going to be billeted at the various schools round about. There was a school at the top of the road where we lived, so we went back home and my father went up to the school to see if he could help. As a result, we had a French officer billeted with us for three or four days. My mother had a brand-new pair of pyjamas that she'd bought for my father; they were hidden away in a drawer, presumably to give him for his next birthday. She lent these pyjamas to the officer. When they left in a rush, his batman came and packed and took the new pyjamas away. I remember my mother being a bit upset about that.

The other thing I remember is that we were the only house in the area that had an immersion heater. It was a newish house – my father had had it built in about 1934 and he'd had an immersion put in – so, unlike those who relied on an old-fashioned boiler, we had plenty of hot water. My father must have said to someone, 'If anyone feels like a bath, do come' and I don't know how many did, but there were a lot of soldiers who one by one came and had a bath at our place. And I can visualise all these men – it was a lovely day – stretched out in the garden asleep. Word got round that they were at our house, and neighbours came with whatever they had – biscuits, cake, milk, bread – so that they could offer them something to eat.

Years later, when I was living in Hertfordshire, I had a neighbour who had been a lieutenant commander in the war and had been at Dunkirk with his ship; he hadn't been able to take his ship right in to the beaches, so it waited offshore while men waded out or were ferried out to it. That explained to me why those uniforms I had seen as a child had been in such a mess.

News of the soldiers returning from Dunkirk quickly spread and became a cause of great excitement. Kate had been evacuated to Ashford, Kent, and on 4 June she wrote home to her parents:

All the soldiers coming home from Dunkirk come through Ashford station. Crowds of people wait along the line for them, to give them refreshments and to collect souvenirs. There are lots of French and Belgians too. They throw lots of things out of the trains. When Doris was there, one threw an old German army boot and Doris claimed a buckle and a piece of leather off the sole.

Bridget remembers a more sombre aspect of the story:

> I knew somebody who only survived Dunkirk because a more experienced sailor on board told him, 'If you have to jump, jump away from the propellers', and he did. Another young man, the son of a neighbour, said they had to leave everything behind, twenty-first birthday presents like cigarette lighters, personal things that were precious to them. Not that it matters in the greater scheme of things, but on a smaller scale it matters enormously.

Not everything that was happening was heroic. A few days later, William, in danger of losing his naval job because of 'reducing manning of certain types of ships engaged in "stationary" war duties', spent a wearisome day in London:

> Squared up Income Tax affairs, net result nothing further to pay for 1939–40. Enquired about new scheme for commission in Air Force. To Admiralty to see about possible job connected with submarines... After lunch to N. S. [National Service] Dept: to see about more active employment re my letter of some 7 weeks previously and not answered. To Min. of Salvage, Savoy Hill. Saw Mr Erridge re saving of waste materials of ships, particularly those in harbours and docks. General impression of visits to various govt. offices and departments is that the inertia, red tape and 'passing the buck' tendencies are our worst enemies.

CHAPTER 5

'MARGARINE AND EGGS
RUNNING DOWN THE STREETS'

Less than three weeks after Dunkirk, France surrendered. Britain (and her various dominions around the world) stood alone. Although Germany had begun to make invasion plans, known as Operation Sea Lion, her leaders were well aware that crossing the Channel would prove both difficult and dangerous. Better, they decided, to initiate a relentless bombing campaign that would force Britain to surrender. The Battle of Britain, which historians date from 10 July to 31 October 1940, was the first – and so far the only – battle to be fought entirely in the air, though of course its effects on the ground were devastating. The nightly bombing of London – which is what many people mean when they talk of 'the Blitz' – didn't begin until early September, but by that time other cities, ports and industrial centres had been under attack for weeks.

Phyllis wrote a piece, published in the *Washington Post* in June 1940, in which she described the stirring events Londoners had lived through in the previous five years, including George V's Jubilee and subsequent death, the abdication of Edward VIII and the Coronation of George VI. She then moved on to wartime:

September, Sunday the 3rd, the solemn words from Downing Street, the air-raid sirens wailing in the empty streets, the pitchy blackness of night ...... and now, June 1940, machine guns, barbed wire, barricades tell us the majestic city stands square to invasion from the skies.

Yet through it all the Londoner seems quite unmoved. He stops to stare at these new fantastic barriers just as three years ago he stopped to stare at the Coronation decorations – with an apparently vague impersonal interest, an expression of lethargic calm. Then he goes on with his usual amusements, ... cafes, pubs and restaurants are crowded out, ... last week London had 43 plays running to New York's 24, evening dresses flutter past the barbed wire, and night clubs don't go home till morning.

But the calm is somewhat illusory. The Londoner feels too much like a fly crawling on the biggest bull's eye in the world. But it's no good getting excited, and the last year or two, and especially the last month or two, have provided such a tale of struggle, betrayal, heroism and disaster, the fantastic coming true, that his battered emotions are getting used up. So he shrugs his shoulders, looks hopefully at the barrage-balloons glittering like jewels above, and hurries resolutely past sand-bagged statues and machine-gun emplacements ...... for in war-time there is only the present tense.

But strain shows in odd ways. Most people are absent-minded, as though their minds were only working on one cylinder ...... they're half-consciously wondering if Italy will come in, what Russia is going to do, whether *he's* in the thick of it out there ...... and there's that perpetual feeling of waiting for something to happen. But the streets and stores are as crowded as ever, only about one person in six carries a gas mask, and in the general air of hushed expectancy there's no hint of despondency.

Vere Hodgson's diaries record her first experience of bombing, in the Notting Hill area:

Tuesday, 25th June 1940: Last night at about 1 a.m. we had the first air raid of the war on London. My room is just opposite the police station, so I got the full benefit of the sirens. I shook all over, but managed to get into my dressing-gown and slippers, put my watch in my pocket, clutch my torch and gas-mask, and get downstairs first. Incidentally I forgot the skylight which is not blacked out, and was rightly reprimanded for showing my torch upwards. I have now covered the light with blue paper and I hope I shall not forget again.

I found myself in a little corridor in which Mrs Gray

was rearing two mattresses against the door. The others gradually assembled. I did not know them and it was dark. I passed round my few bottled sweets. The people chatted and joked.

We could hear no sounds of firing or bombs, so after about a quarter of an hour most of them returned to bed. The two top floorers (myself and another lady) hesitated a few minutes and then we did the same. I looked out the window. The moon was clear and lovely. Not a sound anywhere. I thankfully sank into bed, and eventually fell asleep.

I was awakened by the sirens giving the All Clear; but it was as terrifying as the Alarm, and again I leaped out of bed and donned my dressing-gown. I heard the birds beginning to sing. I saw movement at the police station. A car drove in. At last I realized all was well. I fell asleep once more.

The threat of invasion meant that Sussex was no longer a safe place for evacuated children to be. So, after seven happy months, Jim returned home to South London:

My summer holidays from school in 1940 could best be described as living out the lull before the storm. The air-raid sirens had been sounded twice but, on each occasion, there were no air raids. All four of us were in the house when the fearful sound was heard for the first time, so we quickly got our coats, gas masks and courage, then speedily walked to the shelter. It was a disused railway tunnel that up to now I had never visited. We joined a steady stream of people hurriedly walking across the wasteland behind our home.

Before getting into the shelter we needed to pass beneath an old railway station, giving the entrance to the shelter even greater protection. Two overlapping walls of sandbags about a yard thick provided further protection, and then we were safely inside. Similar sandbag walls secured the entrance at the other end, and half way through the tunnel another pair of overlapping sandbag walls divided the shelter into two sections. With the exception of a direct hit in the centre of the road above, we felt we had total protection. The shelter, although having lights, was totally bare, made even worse when we looked down to find we were standing on earth that had never seen sunshine. There was nowhere to sit and rest, but there was plenty to talk about; in most cases it was a conversation with a total stranger. We stood there for half an hour when a voice near the entrance called out 'All Clear'.

Having spent part of the summer breaking down the fence at the bottom of the garden, allowing easier access to a shelter, Jim had a memorable experience on the Saturday before school was due to start again:

We had only just finished eating when the air-raid siren sounded and Mother took total control. With a true voice of authority, she calmly said, 'We'll do the washing up later, don't run but walk quickly.' Immediately we took my shortcut to the shelter, it was now being used in earnest for the first time. When we got safely inside, we found many people had brought stools, chairs and wooden boxes to sit on. We took up our standing position near the corner of the central sandbag barrier on the old station side. After about half an hour some men came running in, shouting, 'There's a Gerry overhead.' He released five bombs, each one got closer until the final one hit the corner of our shelter at the point where the tunnel's curve was at its deepest.

I had thought an explosion was just a loud bang: what I didn't realise was that all the air disappeared, leaving a vacuum, though the air speedily returned with yet another bang. The sensation cannot be explained in words, but the blast can. It had the effect of lifting the smaller particles of dirt from the ground, creating a dusty form of fog throughout the shelter. Mother grabbed both Ivy and me while all around us kids were screaming and nearly everyone was coughing. A voice came through the dust asking us not to panic and to breathe through our handkerchiefs. Shirts got torn up but most people kept sneezing. Thankfully there were no hysterics at all because, as one lady said, 'We are British.'

While this was happening in London, John was at boarding school in Yorkshire:

I am sure we practised going to the shelters before the first air-raid siren sounded, but from 1940 it became real. The trick was to undress in such a way that underpants were inside trousers, vests inside shirts and socks inside shoes. When the siren sounded, with clothes thus at the ready, even we little ones could file out of our dormitory, led by our Monitor, in under two minutes. Wakefield was not bombed much but it was on the flight paths to Liverpool and Barrow, so over the years we were in the shelters enough times for a routine to develop: a roll call on arrival at the shelters, then, after an interval, organised or encouraged singing and story-telling, lights out if it was a long stay, and (when we were older) surreptitious card games. There was usually hot cocoa when the All Clear sounded. Once, later in the war, a bomber returning home let loose a land-mine to lessen its load. It landed in a near-by field and took out the glass in many of the school's windows. I can still remember how different school noises sounded in glass-less classrooms.

Another John remembers the bombers arriving in Weymouth:

Not long after Dunkirk, my mother and I were sitting in the garden shelling peas and, overhead, there came a solitary German aircraft. It was the first daylight air raid of the war. It didn't drop anything – it was just a reconnaissance flight and it flew quite obviously over the Weymouth harbour area, circled the torpedo factory a couple of times and went away again. At that time – the summer of 1940 – we didn't have any air defences at all; subsequently all along the cliffs there were anti-aircraft gun emplacements. Some of them were real; more of them were imitation, sort of *Blue Peter* concoctions made from drainpipes and boxes with sandbags around them. But it still didn't seem to interfere with how we behaved on a day-to-day basis.

We did get scared, unsurprisingly, during air raids. We all learned to recognise the different engine noises – 'Oh, that's all right, it's one of ours. No, it's one of theirs' – you could hear them coming a long way off. At night, by the time the planes were overhead, there was an incredible noise of anti-aircraft fire, and probably machine-gun fire as well, if we were lucky enough to have any fighters up there. The bombs made a noise as they came down: I don't know if they were specifically designed to do this, but they shrieked. There was a fantastic whistle and you could hear the thing coming down. And in those moments, yes, we were scared. Once you heard them explode you felt a terrible feeling of relief: it wasn't me this time.

Sirens going off were, of course, a regular occurrence. John continues:

The siren was a canister shape, about two and a half feet long, nine or ten inches in diameter, and they were on the top of various buildings around the town – lying on their sides. And presumably they were electrically powered – somebody pressed the button and they went off, all over town.

There was one particularly dramatic occasion:

Once, hearing a bomb, I instinctively dived for cover thinking, 'This is the end.' The all clear hadn't sounded, but everything had gone quiet and I opened the back door to see if there was any action over the Channel. There was an almighty noise behind me, that I thought was a bomb, and I threw myself flat as a German fighter roared over the house and on towards Portland Harbour, clearing the next line of houses by just a few feet. It ended up in the sea about 150 yards from the beach below Sandsfoot Castle. I wondered then, and still do, whether the pilot was trying to save himself by ditching into the sea, or whether he knew he was doomed and bravely used his skills to avoid crashing into our houses – a gallant gentleman like our own precious Few.

Portsmouth was another early target, as Kathy recalls:

When war started I was four years old, living with four adults in Abingdon Road, Portsmouth: I had two brothers, fourteen and seventeen years older than me. There had been no discussion about the forthcoming war, certainly not in front of me – these were 'children should be seen and not heard' days.

I had a number of friends who lived down the road, including one little girl who was so lucky – her mum had a sweet shop. Loving the taste of eight lollies for a halfpenny, I was a frequent customer to my friend's home. The first realisation that something really bad was happening came when I walked up Abingdon Road with my mother to witness the devastation that had occurred during the night. It was a sunny Friday morning in July 1940. Omega Street, where I went to school, and surrounds had been completely wiped out – no school to go to, a complete row of houses and shops now just a smoking pile of bricks. I never saw my friend from the sweet shop again.

That first raid on Portsmouth killed eighteen people and injured a further eighty. Familiar landmarks such as the Blue Anchor Hotel were devastated, while a bomb on a local gasholder caused damage that took 1,500 steel plates to repair. A second and third raid a month later destroyed St John's Church and severely damaged a cinema that was showing a film to an audience consisting largely of children. In total well over one humdred people were killed and many hundreds were rendered homeless. As Kathy puts it, 'These were the scenes my five-year-old eyes witnessed: street upon street of devastation.' Her story continues:

I learned very quickly that if a siren sounded during the day we were to rush out into the garden and make ourselves comfortable in the Anderson shelter. But just in case a siren sounded if you were caught out in the city, most street corners had a brick shelter that could accommodate plenty of people – maybe about thirty to fifty. My dad had a long journey to get home from work over at the ordnance depot in Gosport – it was right round the other side of the harbour from where we lived – and he had to run from shelter to shelter if he was caught up in a raid. As soon as he was close enough to home, he would call out to my mother to open the shelter door and he would run as fast as he could to get inside, thus giving me a chance to have a look at the sky outside, which was full of searchlights weaving all over the place. The noise didn't frighten me at all. I grabbed every opportunity to have a nosy at what was going on. The white searchlights, red sky and the noise of the sky battle – I just took them all in with a sort of childlike wonder. Every morning after a bad night, I would borrow my brother Chris's tin ARP helmet and collect shrapnel that had fallen during the night.

As the nightly sky battles worsened, I was never put to bed in my upstairs bedroom. It was far easier to go to bed in the garden shelter, as it was inevitable that the German Air Force would bomb Portsmouth, a naval city, under cover of darkness.

It's strange to remember all the things that I just took for granted. The young can absorb horrible things that would give an adult a severe meltdown, I am sure of it. My adult family around me – Mum, Dad, Chris at home and John away in the navy – never ever talked to me about what was happening; I didn't know who Churchill was; Hitler was a bad man who lived far, far away. John gave his life with hundreds of others when HMS *Gloucester* sank in the Battle of Crete in 1941 and not until long after the end of the war did anyone explain to me why my big brother never came home again. It was, it seems, a forbidden subject.

As the bombing worsened, Kathy was evacuated to a nearby village:

A first taste of peace came upon me – I heard birds singing in the trees and I had no worries at all. In the four years I stayed there, there was only one bomb, which accidentally landed in a field, hurting no one.

In Luton, on the afternoon of 30 August 1940, all that time Herbert had spent playing dominoes and solo whist suddenly acquired a purpose:

Then it happened. A faint throbbing drone in a clear blue sky. People doing their shopping. A louder roar of engines. A thin whistle rising to a shriek. A sharp crack. A cloud of smoke. A moment when all life stood still, and then the wailing of the siren and the drift of people to the shelters. No rushing, no panic, just a line of human beings waiting to go downstairs. A policeman still standing on point duty directing traffic to the side of the road. Broken glass everywhere and more wails followed by bangs and roars and smoke. Men leaving work with tin hats and respirators. Warden 464 reporting. Post T1 fully manned. All men on patrol.

'Take shelter please' – and then quiet. They have gone. Three minutes after the first wallop there is left nothing left but ruined houses, white-faced children with frightened looks in their eyes. Women at the front gates of houses, with their eyes gazing down the street. For the Works had got a packet. The smoke from an oil fire drifts high into the sky. An ambulance clangs down the street. My first air raid and, as I bandage a kid's arm, I swear, and swear, and swear.

So the initiation into the closeness of modern war. Training, drilling and making myself acquainted with the people of my sector had been done for this. To stand and bandage a ten-year-old boy's arm, whose hand tightly clutched a two-shilling piece – 'For Muvver said I mustn't lose it.'

I felt like crying – and I did.

John in Weymouth had hardly been affected by the first months of the war, but he remembers that when the Battle of Britain got underway, things did change:

Portland Bill sticks out into the Channel in such a way that it was used as a landmark, a navigational aid, for German bombers, principally on their way to Coventry. So they used to fly overhead on the way to the Midlands and if they had any bombs left on the way home, they used to drop them on Weymouth. The Germans didn't have radar, so this sort of landmark was important to them.

There weren't many daylight raids, but when there were there were dogfights and we could stand out in the garden and watch them, almost like a performance – we could see the planes pursuing each other, vapour trails in the sky. I don't remember being frightened – even with a dogfight over my head, it all seemed rather remote and most of the time I think we were more curious than frightened. We used to go out after air raids and pick up bits of shrapnel. Some of them would still be hot.

There was a lot of activity at night, though, including deliberate targeting of the two sections of the torpedo facility – the factory and the testing area. But it was so entertaining, I would stand upstairs and watch: sometimes they caught a plane in the searchlights and tried to shoot it down, but not often very successfully. We didn't have any lights on, so it was perfectly OK to stand there in the dark, peeping out through the blackout curtains. One night I was watching a landmine floating down on a parachute, towards the torpedo testing area. But I didn't get to watch it land because one of the commandos who was billeted with us came up and said, 'John, you'd better get in the shelter', so I had to go downstairs and out into the garden.

The mine landed within yards of the torpedo testing area. It was through the resulting wreckage that I subsequently walked to school every day. In fact, my school was so damaged during that raid that we couldn't go to school for a while and we were relocated to the old Weymouth College, just on the edge of the harbour.

The arrangements for evacuating the school during air raids were very *Dad's Army* and ineffective. There were some trenches that had been built about a mile from the school, and as the air-raid warning sounded, we formed a crocodile and walked off towards the trenches. I don't think we ever got there before the all clear was sounded and we turned round and walked back again.

David, who had come back to Beckenham from the safety of Devon towards the end of 1939, found himself in danger the following summer:

Coming out of Cubs (Cub Scouts as they call them today), we could see over Biggin Hill and Croydon aerodromes. Over both those places we could see dogfights in the sky. To a ten-year-old boy it was wonderful. I was gazing up in amazement when a very inconsiderate woman came and dragged me away – that was my mother.

At night-time, looking towards London you could see the fires over the docks and a red glow in the sky. There was a lot of bombing around where we lived. I suppose it was good (from the German point of view) to drop bombs either on the way to London, because of the anti-aircraft defences, or on the way back, just to discharge them. Our Cub hut was completely destroyed towards the end of that summer and our house was only about fifty yards from there. We were blasted out; we would have been killed if we'd been in our beds, but we were in the Anderson shelter, which my dad had put in. It had a lovely concrete lining, so I suppose it was reasonably safe.

The ARP were pretty good – they came round to see that we were OK. Dad had got a bang on his head but, apart from that, we weren't hurt. The following morning, my school teacher, a lovely lady, also took the trouble to come to see if we were all right and to advise my mother that there were shelters near where she lived, where we could go for a few days. So we did that while Dad got in contact with relatives again, to arrange for us to go back to Devon. The previous time he had taken us by car, but now petrol was short and we went by train from Paddington. I remember waiting on the station and there being some nuns in the tea place; in my child's mind I thought, 'Well, we'll be safe if we stay near these nuns.'

London, and the suburbs of London where we lived, were a real hell: there was gloom, dust, bombs, noise. Before we were bombed, while we were at school, we spent hours in shelters, shouting out our times tables or singing songs in order to cover up the noise of gunfire. It was a horrible time.

June in Andover, Hampshire, thinks back to that summer with more enthusiasm:

I was only ten when we had the Battle of Britain. There was nothing like it, really – particularly when you're only ten. The main feeling I remember was excitement. We saw planes come in and drop bombs on RAF Andover: that was 13 August 1940; I saw them from the High Street. I was shopping with my mother when the siren went off. We were used to seeing aeroplanes, but suddenly realised that these were enemy raiders, circling to the west of town, in the direction of the aerodrome. Just then, my mother exclaimed, 'What's that? Is it a parachute?' An Australian soldier standing nearby answered, 'No, they're bombs, ma'am.'

Remember that aeroplanes couldn't get into the stratosphere in those days – I think they fought at about 15,000 feet, so you could see them quite clearly. The Spitfires used the famous Merlin engines and they sounded different from anything else; everyone recognised that engine noise. But we watched the fighting, too – I remember seeing one plane heading back to base with smoke streaming out of it; it had obviously been hit.

It was exciting – when you're ten years old, you don't worry about things like that, unless you actually get hurt.

Seven-year-old Wendy was another who found it all quite exciting:

We lived in Surrey on the edge of the North Downs, which was relatively safe, though I do remember summer air raids when I was out with my siblings. The siren went off and we were all ordered off the streets into the underground shelter at the bus terminal; we stayed till the all clear sounded.

During the Battle of Britain we frequently saw German airmen bailing out of the summer sky from their burning planes and a great fear – I was seven – was that they would come into the house at night and attack me. Sometimes in order to make a quick getaway from the anti-aircraft guns they would jettison their bombs over the Downs and head for home. From time to time playing on the Downs we would find bomb craters in the chalky landscape.

Connie was in Liverpool:

My mother wouldn't let me be evacuated because there were tales of children who were in homes that weren't very nice. So she said, 'No. If we're going to die, we can all die together.' But we got through the war and here I am now with three grandsons and seven great-grandchildren.

Before the Blitz started we used to take ferries across the Mersey, to the seaside at New Brighton, where there was a fairground, too. It was threepence to go to Seacombe, another seaside place, and sixpence for New Brighton – that was the place to go. But the ferryboats started to get bombed, because of course Liverpool was an important port and they were after the ships and the warehouses. The Lancaster bombers flew very low – not all that much higher than the rooftops. You could see them so clearly in the sky. We'd go into the parks and see the searchlights and as children we would think, 'Oh, isn't that marvellous?' until we were chased away by the air-raid wardens.

For about a week it seemed it never stopped bombing. It was nothing to see ropes across the end of the street with signs saying, 'Unexploded bomb'. We took it for granted, we'd just walk past. But I do remember going into town one morning and seeing margarine and eggs running down the streets, because a food warehouse had been hit. I said to my mother, 'Isn't this awful?' and she said, 'Well, never mind, because we're all rationed today.' For most of the First World War there hadn't been rationing, so the rich could buy all the food up and the poor would just be left. In the Second World War, we may have been short of things, but in theory at least it was fair – everyone was in the same boat.

All this was in the summer of 1940. After a renewed Blitz at Christmas, Liverpool had a respite of several months, but then the Luftwaffe (German air force) struck again. Connie continues:

In July 1941, my sister was working in an insurance office in Castle Street, not all that far from the Pier Head. During the Blitz, Castle Street was flattened – absolutely gone. Everything was gone. That night my sister was missing and my father was going up the wall:

'Where is she? I'm going out to look for her.'

My mother said, 'You can't go out to look for her – the wardens won't let you go anywhere.'

Anyway, she was all right. She had been in the air-raid shelter at the Pier Head: she'd been waiting for a tram car to bring her home when the sirens went. At the bottom of the street was a big statue of Queen Victoria and she wasn't touched. It was a bit like that famous picture of St Paul's surrounded by flames. Queen Victoria was surrounded by rubble, but all the same it was very symbolic.

Where the buildings had been they later built big square tanks, which they filled with water to put the fires out when the bombs came down. Even today there are shrapnel marks on the walls of the Town Hall.

On the other side of the Mersey, Joan's family had an extraordinary experience, benefiting from the kindness of strangers. They were living in Wallasey and used to watch the bombs over Liverpool:

One night, my mother decided we should go into the shelter and, when we came out, we discovered that we had an unexploded bomb in the garden. That had to be dealt with and whatever they did to the bomb made our house uninhabitable. So my mother went around, with her two small daughters (my sister and me), looking for someone to take us in. She literally went from house to house asking for help. We ended up in Heswall, on the other side of the Wirral from Wallasey, so goodness knows how many doors Mum had knocked on before we got there. We were taken in, as a family, by complete strangers and we stayed with them for the rest of the war – nearly five years.

Bombing wasn't confined to the cities and ports. In rural Suffolk, John's mother had 'an experience' at the start of the Blitz:

She and a friend were working at cutting down the thistles in the marshes by the river, so that the cows could get in there to graze. On this particular day the Germans came over and bombed Martlesham Heath, the local airbase. They'd followed the river up from the coast, which is only about ten miles away – they knew where they were going. Mother and her friend flung themselves into a ditch until the planes had passed over. She told us afterwards that the bombers had been flying so low that she could see the people in them.

Anne was in Newport, South Wales:

They very often dropped odd bombs that they hadn't used on their real targets further north, when they were on their way back home to Germany. We lived on the highest hill in Newport, the Ridgeway, and one night a bomb was dropped near us and it hit a gas main. For four days a column of flame was burning and – this will tell you how daft we were – I reckon everyone in Newport went up to look at it. It was like a procession. I even remember my mother pushing me up there in the pushchair. It must have been terribly dangerous.

In August 1940, Phyllis had been attending a summer school in Devon, returning to London just as the Blitz was starting. She kept a diary that she called *Journal under the Terror*.

Tuesday September 3rd. Today, I returned to London to find it apparently unchanged in spite of the frequent air-raid warnings. Familiarity has bred contempt, and the heart-chilling wail of the siren has been followed so often by a deathly silence that it now means little. The streets remain crowded, lovers wander arm-in-arm, children play their games, men tend to their gardens, undisturbed. It all shows what custom will do.

Wednesday September 4th. A German bomber is hovering above my top-floor room as I write these words. I recognise the peculiar hiccoughing noise of its engines, which sound directly above. A cautious reconnaissance has shown me a sky criss-crossed with powerful searchlights which meet in brilliant circles above, and are reflected in all the surrounding windows. There are thuds of gunfire and distant flashes suggesting a fireworks display; somewhere overhead a deadly load is poised in bomb racks.

A month ago, the very thought would have filled me

with abject terror – in fact, the first time that I found myself in just this situation my teeth chattered with fright. As we crouched beneath the stairs listening to the sinister roar of aeroplane engines through the night and the distant crumps of bombs, my morale was poor and my thoughts about our 'civilisation' bitter. The blessed notes of the 'all clear' sounded like a reprieve from Hell. But the next night it happened all over again, and the next, and when nothing worse succeeded, we all grew rapidly more nonchalant. We recalled that aeroplanes always sound directly overhead whether they are or no, and that gunfire is heard scores of miles away. Now I am so accustomed to German machines that I can stay up here and write in spite of them.

Friday, September 6th. Today, I attended a Promenade Concert at the Queen's Hall, where the entire ground-floor space is given up to standing-room. It was a Beethoven concert, and although the warning had gone, the entire hall was packed with a mammoth audience. On to a theatre, where a further warning had no effect on a big audience, and then to a restaurant jam-packed with jovial beings and home through streets whizzing with traffic under an impressive display of searchlights.

Saturday, September 7th. Tonight, I emerged from a riotous entertainment at the Holborn Empire to find all London lit up with a vivid apricot glow from fires in the east, a glow that turned the stabbing searchlight beams to violet and blackly silhouetted every spire and tower. There were ominous thuds and bangs from every side, and A. A. [anti-aircraft] shells flashed up above where the searchlights crossed. We decided on a quick return home, and hadn't been in the house long before we made a quicker descent to the shelter.

A young fireman named F W Hurd, attached to Euston Road Fire Station, was on duty on that Saturday night:

London had been subjected to 'nuisance' raids for about a month. The warning would sound, usually just after dark, and occasional planes would be heard droning over (we soon became adept at distinguishing the peculiar rise and fall note of German engines). The object of these 'raids' was presumably to disorganise transport and production and make things awkward in general. This latter it certainly did for us in the Fire Service. As soon as the warning went, we were required to rig ourselves in full fire gear with respirator at the 'alert', and to stay rigged until the 'all-clear' sounded. No joke this when the warning usually lasted from middle evening till the early hours of the morning. (This order for rigging was later rescinded, it being necessary to don full gear only on leaving cover.)

On this particular day, Saturday 7th Sept 1940, the sirens had wailed their warning at about 4.30 pm. We heard planes and later a dog-fight could be discerned well away to the east. We also saw parachutes descending through the puffs of A. A. smoke. 'Over the Thames again,' we said. (The Estuary and parts of the riverside up from there had been enduring raids for some time.) After a short time, it was no longer possible to distinguish the planes at all, the sky being apparently empty except for a few scattered shell bursts. We entered our shelter (a room on the ground floor) and settled down to await the all clear and supper, which would be served about 6.30. We were getting a bit fed up with this sort of thing and I think a few of us (I know I did) half-hoped for 'something to happen' and then felt ashamed for letting the monotony 'get us down'.

Then suddenly it came! The alarm bell rang at 6.15. All pumps (two heavy units and four trailer pumps) were ordered to Kingsland Road Station to 'stand-by'. The all-clear sounded as we pushed across the 'Angel' junction. Long before we reached Kingsland Road, we could see a vast column of smoke rising into the sky. I myself was riding the 1st Heavy, and standing along the sides of that we had an uninterrupted view.

From Kingsland Road they were instructed to proceed to East Ham:

This station, although in the London Fire Region, is outside the LCC area and we all guessed it must be something unusual to send us from Euston on a journey that long.

As soon as we entered the East End we saw evidence of the raids (the first most of us had seen). Houses were demolished, roads torn up, and a surface shelter had been wrecked. Ambulance and rescue squads were at work as we passed. Fires of varying size were visible all round. Arrived at East Ham, my pump was ordered to visit several addresses where incendiary bombs had been reported. As it happened, these had all been extinguished by wardens and civilians. We returned to East Ham Station just at 'black-out' time, and after a few minutes, the sirens sounded again.

Shortly afterwards, they were ordered to Becton Gas Works, where 'chaos met our eyes':

Gasometers were punctured and were blazing away, a power house had been struck, rendering useless the hydraulic hydrant supply (the only source of water there). An overhead gantry bearing lines of trucks communicating with the railway siding was also well alight. And then, overhead, we heard 'Jerry'. The searchlights were searching the sky in a vain effort to locate him. Guns started firing, and then I had my first experience of a bomb explosion. A weird whistling sound and I ducked beside the pump, together with two more of the crew... Then a vivid flash of flame, a column of earth and debris flying into the air, and the ground heaved. I was thrown violently against the side of the appliance. As 'he' still concentrated his attentions on our fire we were forced to take shelter in the works 'dug-out'. After a time, things quietened down, and we went out again. It was now about 10 o/c and the fire had been burning unattacked by us for lack of water. At that time a Local Fire Officer arrived and informed us that he knew where we could obtain a supply! Our 'heavy' was sent about a half mile from the fire to 'pick up' water from three other pumps, which were being supplied from hydrants. We relayed the water through a chain of pumps to the fire.

Out there, with nothing to do except watch the hose and guard it where it crossed an arterial road (from being burst by cars proceeding at speed across it), we had time to look round. What a sight. About a mile away to our right was the riverfront. The whole horizon on that side was a sheet of flame. The docks were afire! On all other sides it was much the same. Fires everywhere. The sky was a vivid orange glow. And all the time the whole area was being mercilessly bombed. The road shuddered with the explosions. A. A. shells were bursting overhead. A Royal Navy Destroyer berthed in one of the docks was firing her A. A. equipment, as were other ships. The shrapnel literally rained down.

It was now about midnight and, still, this incessant racket kept on. It surprised me how quickly one got used to sensing whether a bomb was coming our way or not. At first, we all lay flat every time we heard anything but, after an hour or so, we only dived for it if one came particularly close. Even so, I had a funny feeling inside each time *I* heard it coming. (It took quite a time to overcome that. It wasn't exactly fear, but I don't know now just what it was.)

At about 3.30 a.m. a canteen van arrived and served us our tea and sandwiches. It was the first 'bite' any of us had had since 1 o/c midday the day before, 14½ hours ago. Just then the bombing became more severe and localised. A brighter glow was in the sky immediately over us, then we saw the flames. They had started another fire in the gas works, which by now, after about six hours' concentrated work by us on it, had been got well under control. Then a huge mushroom of flame shot into the air from the docks, followed by a dull rolling roar. An oil container had exploded. The whole atmosphere became terrible again with the noise of gunfire. (Afterwards, when London established its famous barrage, we got used to it, but on that first night, it was just hell.)

Then, quite suddenly, it ceased. The silence was almost over-powering for a time. Then, about 5 o/c a.m., the 'all clear' went. We had been subjected without any real cover to 8 hours' bombing.

Phyllis's journal for the following day confirms how grim that night was:

Sunday, September 8th. Last night was a night of horror, a hell on earth. About one o'clock, I heard the sound of an approaching bomb for the first time, an appalling shriek like a train whistle growing nearer and nearer, and then a sickening crash reverberating through the earth. At intervals through the night we heard the same dread sound, and each time as we held our breaths in relief at our own escape, we knew that somewhere else at hand agony and horror had struck.

Sybilla in Ealing, West London, whose father was German, recalls the same period:

Ealing seemed relatively safe at first. One thing that brought home the extent of the Blitz on London Docks and the East End was the sight of all the taxis, lorries and fire-service vehicles standing charred, and fire hoses hanging up to dry, at the garage where Yates Wine Lodge now stands. During one particularly heavy air raid we were sheltering downstairs under an iron bed frame balanced on two tables and with a mattress on top. Amidst the noise we heard a tapping at the window. It was an ARP patrol warning of a possible evacuation of the area as several unexploded incendiary bombs had landed in the churchyard. With the blackout in force, we tiptoed our way carefully towards the front of the shop, hoping to avoid the shattered glass we were sure would be everywhere. Yet although the shop had two huge plate-glass windows, they were still intact. Virtually every window in the parade and opposite was smashed except ours. This was the cause of much merriment locally, that the German shop was unscratched. The blast effect from bombs was unpredictable.

Sylvia was a bit farther west:

> We were living in Slough when the Blitz started. I
> remember very clearly that my parents had gone for
> a drink. We had petrol – my father was entitled to it
> because of his work, which was something secret. I
> genuinely never knew what it was, because he didn't talk
> about it, but it sometimes took him far enough away that
> he needed to drive: I remember he had to go to Bristol
> once to inspect the damage after a heavy raid, but I don't
> know any more than that. Anyway, on this occasion we
> had gone out in a car and my younger sister and I were
> left in the back of the car with some nuts and raisins or
> crisps or something while my parents went and had a
> drink. They came out of the pub and I said, 'There's a
> sunset, but it's in the wrong place.' My father looked at
> the sky to the east and said, 'That's London.' We could
> see the red glow from as far away as Slough. That's how
> I became aware that the bombing had started.

Shirley, at primary school near Biggin Hill in Kent, remembers
a dramatic moment around the same time:

> My sister and I were coming out of school one day;
> it was about midday, one o'clock, we must have been
> going home for lunch. We saw my father running
> towards us. He was a rather plump man and we were
> at first astonished by his speed. Then when he reached
> us, he flung us into the nearest hedge – somebody else's

hedge, just a few bushes that separated their garden from the road. We couldn't imagine what he was up to. And suddenly there was a plane that came down and went, 'Ah-ah-ah-ah-ah.' So we weren't indignant any more. That was the closest we came to the action – but it was really quite close!

Seven-year-old Paul's mother was involved in various aspects of war work during the London Blitz:

In 1940, I went to prep school for the first time and in the summer holidays I came back home, which at that time was Hampstead Garden Suburb. Opposite our house was a golf course that had been turned into an anti-aircraft site. It had enormous guns on it. Next to the house was an empty site, because the Suburb hadn't been fully developed at that stage, and one of the great sports was to go out in the morning and pick up the bits and pieces of shells and shrapnel and stuff that had come down during the night.

The Battle of Britain was just starting. My mother and her friend Connie did various things: first of all, they joined the ARP and trained to go round picking up people's legs and arms that, they were told, were going to fall off at any minute during the air raids. They told me about one time when they were all dressed up in their protective gear, with gas masks on, in a van, driving around, looking for people to rescue, and they got sandwiched into a funeral cortège going from St

John's Wood to Golders Green. They couldn't get out of it, so they had to go on, solemnly processing, with their gas masks on. Whether they ever did pick up any stray limbs, I don't know, but I don't think so.

After a while they stopped doing that and trained to take samples from the water stations. I used to go on these trips with them. Again, they were given a van to do it in. It was a great luxury to go anywhere in a petrol-driven vehicle. They went to all the various pumping stations: there was one at Victoria, another one at Chiswick, one down in Bromley, I think – all over the place. And they took water samples because there was a fear that the water supply was going to be poisoned by the Germans.

One of their enterprises I remember most vividly was a canteen that they ran for fire-fighters in the Blitz. My mother was a musician and she was linked to the London Philharmonic Orchestra, which is not relevant to the story except that the orchestra was absolutely on its uppers and broke, so Mamma and Connie ran this canteen for the benefit of the orchestra. They set up a van and charged a penny for a cup of tea and a halfpenny for a bun, or something like that, to all the people fighting the fires in the City. Occasionally, if it wasn't too dangerous, I was taken along on these trips. I remember one time when we were going down Paddington Street in Marylebone, and of course at that age – seven – the horrors of the war don't mean anything. It was a complete adventure, very exciting. There was a baker's on the corner; it was on fire and I remember saying to my mother, 'Won't that be a lot of lovely toast!'

Paul's mother may never have had to pick up a limb, but Sheila's mother, an ARP warden in the East End, did:

When the siren went off, she had to go round and make sure that everyone was in a safe place – in the Anderson shelter in their garden, or down the Tube or in one of those brick shelters they had in the middle of the road, and she had terrible stories – she was once hit round the face by a hand that had been blown off someone who'd been killed.

Marjorie's father, another ARP warden, had a less violent but nonetheless poignant experience:

He used to do twenty-four hours on, twenty-four hours off. I remember once when he had been out all night, he came home in the morning and told us that he had been to a house where the breakfast table had been laid for the morning, but a bomb had dropped in the night and the people had been killed.

In September 1940, disaster struck Canning Town in the East End of London. Sheila remembers:

My future husband George lived in the Plaistow area, and his family used to go under the railway arches to shelter. Lots of people would pile in there and on one occasion, there were so many that one of the air-raid wardens said it was dangerous, they'd have to take some people out. So they called out the names of a few streets and told anyone who lived in those streets to go to a different place for safety. They took them round to a local school. George's father was an air-raid warden helping out and he was one of those who took all those families away from the arches and into the school.

That night there was a particularly bad raid and some children had pulled down a blackout curtain in the school, so the window was lit up and it got struck. A lot of the people inside were killed. And of course the air-raid wardens felt terrible, because they'd been the ones who took them round there. There's a big memorial to them in the cemetery in Canning Town, because they all died together.

George's father was there the next day, helping to dig the bodies out – it must have been dreadful. He was never right after that; he was always ill and he died when he was only in his late forties or early fifties.

It was kept secret for many years, but the Canning Town tragedy is now known to have been one of the worst disasters involving civilians in the whole course of the Second World War: the number of dead was close to 600.

Away from the main targets, stray bombs caused their share of damage. Sam remembers them in North London:

The cupboard under the stairs was a little triangular affair, only as deep as the width of the staircase. It's where we kept some raffia floor mats that somebody must have given my parents as a wedding present, along with the carpet sweeper (we couldn't afford a vacuum cleaner) and small household stuff like old pillows and cushions. My mother used to take my sister and me to sit under there quite regularly. It was probably the safest place – I should think it would have taken a direct hit to demolish the staircase and kill us. What comes back to me most clearly when I think of this is the smell of all the bits and pieces in that cupboard, which of course had acquired their own aroma over the years. It was a combination of rubber and dust and mildew and decay; if I were to smell it again it would bring the whole experience back to me. But it was very exciting for small children, sitting on the floor, crouched down in our mother's arms.

I remember sitting there in the dark, with the noise of the bombers overhead. We didn't hear bombs dropping except on one occasion and that was a few hundred yards away. We were a long way from the main Blitz area – if we got any bombs it was because a member of the Luftwaffe happened to be on his way home and realised he still had a bomb left in the belly. That's what happened to the house a few hundred yards from us, which was severely damaged. I remember going out in the middle of the night and looking at the plume of smoke coming up from the end of the road.

Margaret was in Walthamstow, Essex:

I think it was in 1941 that we had a land mine dropped very close to us. It wiped out at least a third of the road. In the middle of the road was a large Presbyterian church, a very solid building, and anything on one side of it was destroyed. We were lucky because we were on the other side and, although we had all our windows blown out, the house stayed intact.

After that I had to do fire watching, because there were so few people left to do it. We weren't given protective clothing or anything, but my father still had his tin hat from the First World War, so I wore that. As well as looking after our road, I fire watched at the local maternity hospital. There was a sort of shelter and you were given blankets. After the first night I went home covered in spots and my mother said, 'Good heavens, they're bed bugs!' Of course, they'd been in the blankets. Nobody had seemed to think they ought to be washed.

Billy remembers an incident in Bathgate, West Lothian:

Three bombs were dropped one night in the field at Whiteside, less than a mile from us. The boggy ground absorbed the explosion – none of the slates were even blown off the roofs of the miners' cottages nearby. But a fourth bomb landed at the North British Steel Foundry across the road, and when I woke up in the morning, I soon learned that the war had come to Bathgate. In no time I was making a beeline for the site, over fence, through marsh and mud field.

My concept of a bombed field was coloured by the images I had seen in my dad's First World War book. I was actually disappointed. Three neat round holes, albeit large, ran in line down the field towards the factory. They were filled to the brim with water. The water table below the marshy ground had saved the houses, and the Town Council had 'sanitised' my only bit of war devastation by putting a wire-and-post fence round each. Maybe this was the first example of health and safety in Bathgate.

The story goes that Hitler didn't want Blackpool to be bombed because he intended it to remain a holiday resort after he invaded (folklore also maintains that Oxford was spared because it was to be his capital). Irvine, ten years old when the raids started, remembers that Blackpool didn't escape completely:

Aunty Madeline was sitting in the living room, a cup of tea in her lap, as the first bombs came whistling down. In a startling dive she flung herself across the floor and crashed in among us children sheltering under the stairs. Hot tea everywhere as explosions shattered around the factory in the brickworks behind our house. Our row of homes escaped direct hits, but from that night on it became a family joke that the Germans had bombed us with pots of tea.

It was summer of 1940; many people feared that Britain would soon be invaded and the Germans would win the war. It was a frightening thought.

The local factory, which had switched from manufacturing buses to making aircraft parts, escaped being destroyed, but night after night now we heard the drone of German bombers high overhead, flying north across Morecambe Bay to bomb the shipyards at Barrow-in-Furness. We lost count of how many planes.

The threat of bombing resulted in some rapid action at the factory. Men set about camouflaging the vast grey roof. Everyone realised what an easy target it was. Spider-like, the men crawled across it, painting large black, green and tan patterns. It still stood out in daylight, but was less obvious by moonlight.

Outside our house, in the street, a group of men put on steel helmets and formed the Colwyn Avenue Air Raid Warden Unit. Their helmets were unlike anything that soldiers wore. They had a curled edge and we kids thought they looked comical, but the wardens still wore them. Years later, Granddad's became a flower pot in the back garden.

The wardens began practising how to put out fires from imaginary incendiary bombs. Mr Thompson, a councillor who liked to be in charge, appointed himself chief warden. Granddad, a former engineer, was ordered to make sure the stirrup pumps worked; other men were told to ensure the sand buckets were full; we kids were instructed not to come near.

As it was summer the wardens practised every evening, but if nothing significant happened, they gradually began to stand around in the road talking. Our gang decided to liven things up. Secretly, we made a bomb of our own – a bundled mix of rags and paper. We waited for the right evening and when no one seemed to be watching, we propped it against a garage door, doused it in petrol and threw a lighted match. We ran for it as the petrol burst into flames.

'A bomb! A bomb!' we yelled.

The startled fire-fighters tumbled about and the stirrup-pump men soon put out the flames. The garage owner complained angrily to the wardens for damaging the paint on his garage door. One of our gang, Young Bill, caught too close to the flames, had his eyebrows singed and his mother stormed around to our houses and told us off. We tried to blame it on the war, but none of us was allowed to attend another practice.

It took more than that to deter Irvine, Young Bill and the rest of the gang, however:

We decided instead that our back lane needed protecting. It was behind my house and was a quagmire in winter, but a great playground in the summer.

We dug a deep hole in the middle of the lane and disguised it with a covering of branches. The plan was to catch a German Panzer tank. Unfortunately, a policeman stumbled into our tank trap and, amid some scorching

words, we were ordered to refill it. The branches had
fallen into the hole and the policeman stood over us
while we dragged them out, then shovelled the soil back
in. It was wet, heavy clay, so that was hard work. The
policeman threatened to have us in court if we ever
did anything so silly again, but it was really the fear of
having to fill in another hole that stopped us repeating
the performance.

The trap had been dug near a large garden full of
apple trees. They were laden with fruit. An old man
lived there but, though we tried, we never managed to
raid the garden. He was too watchful and as a result
we called him the Mean Miser. A day came when the
roads filled with hundreds of evacuees escaping the
London bombing and being found emergency homes.
To our surprise the miser called us into the garden
and told us to strip his orchard of all the apples and to
share them out among the evacuees in our street. And
that's what we did. There were baskets and baskets of
apples and from that day forward we called the old man
the Kind Miser.

Like most country folk, Joan, a Londoner living in rural
Northamptonshire, escaped the nightly bombardments, but
had the occasional freak incident:

There was hardly any trouble in Northamptonshire
from the Blitz, but while we were in London, from
what I gathered afterwards, a rogue plane that had been

bombing further over was coming back with one bomb on board and jettisoned it in the field behind where we lived. My dad said afterwards it was damned silly – everyone had told him that if he sent me back to the London area I'd be killed, but in fact if I'd stayed at home I'd have been killed, because the blast took the back of our house out and my bed went through the window and finished up at right angles on top of the shed. So despite the fact that I was in Southall with all the Battle of Britain going on all around me, one rogue bomb in Northamptonshire would have killed me.

Dad got the windows and everything repaired, but for ages afterwards there was a crack right the way down the wall, across the landing and up the stairs – that wasn't repaired until after the war.

In mid-1941, the war took a different turn. Although bombs had rained down on British cities and ports for over eight months, there was no sign of a surrender; despite the widespread damage to factories, production of the materials needed for war actually increased. Germany adopted a new strategy. Bombing of mainland Britain virtually ceased as the Luftwaffe's efforts were once more directed against the supply convoys in the Atlantic. And, in a continuing effort to expand German *Lebensraum* (living space), Hitler had also turned his attention towards the east. Phyllis wrote in her journal:

Sunday June 22nd.
Hitler invaded Russia this morning. Well, we've sure

got a powerful new ally. One thing is certain, the Russians won't give up like the French, because they've got something they believe in to fight for.

I worked in the office till lunch time and then joined six others from the Settlement in a crazy cycling expedition. It was the hottest day of the year, well up in the nineties, and there we were, peddling along a blistering main road with our wheels sticking fast to the melting tar.

We had supper in a hotel at Westerham whilst we listened to Winston's speech. It was grand – he is so superbly single-minded about the war. And how effective to say at once that we are wholeheartedly with Russia, and not hesitate a couple of weeks before making a grudging decision. We lingered so long listening to his speech that it was nine-thirty before we set off with another sixteen miles to go. It was the longest day in the year, but it wasn't long enough for us, and we arrived at Croydon at twenty to twelve (with no lights on our bikes) to find that we had missed the last train. That meant a hotel, where Joan and I shared a ferociously hot room. As we had no night things we just went to bed without anything on. No sooner had we sunk upon our beds than a plane came over and the warning went. We felt obliged to get up and put on our clothes, then it got quiet and we took them off again. The guns immediately started, and we put them on again. It got quiet and we took them off again. Another plane came over and we put them on again, and so on for a couple of hours, all in pitch darkness except for the gun flashes, as we had de-blacked out. All in all, we didn't get much sleep.

We had to catch an early train (a businessman's special in which our shorts were coldly regarded) and by this time the female members of the party were so exhausted that we returned from Victoria in a taxi with the bicycles on top – placed so that the bells rang continuously all the way – an odd end to our cycling expedition. But what fun it was.

A week or so later, Vere Hodgson wrote:

Wednesday 2nd July 1941: Feel much better this week. Very hot. A jar of honey has been given me. Very pleasant to receive. Able to get one whole pound of tomatoes without queuing for them – so Hitler is not having it all his own way.

The Blitz may have been over, but Margaret remembers:

When the bombing stopped, for several nights you couldn't sleep, because you were so used to the noise of the anti-aircraft guns and the planes that when it was silent, you really could not get to sleep. It was quite weird.

CHAPTER 6

'NO GAS OR ELECTRICITY, AND ONE TAP OVER THE KITCHEN SINK'

For many children away from the big cities and ports, life during the war carried on much as usual. Those too young to grasp what was going on remember sunny summer days, cycle rides and picnics, but very little fear or deprivation. Hazel, aged ten when war broke out and living in Barnstaple in North Devon, was one of them:

> We heard a few planes going overhead on their way to South Wales, but that was about it. My father was too old for active service, so he remained at home. There were obviously foods that you couldn't get, but we never went hungry. Entertainment in the evening was the radio or cards.
>
> As for the holidays, I remember cycling down to the beach, to Saunton Sands, about ten miles away, as I

would have done before the war. There was very little traffic, if any, and we could spread across the road, seven or eight of us abreast. When we reached Saunton there was a steep road down to the beach and we used to leave our bicycles at the top – no thought that they would be stolen! We then found a place on the beach and remained for the rest of the day, in and out of the sea, and home in the early evening.

If the weather was not good we'd go a bit further, to Croyde Bay, and walk along a very narrow path past the headland to the end, where there were lots of birds nesting.

On Fridays during school holidays I would go to the local market with my mother to collect her 'farm' butter [rationed] and other things. Farmers' wives used to come to the market with big wicker baskets, which they opened to make a stall and display their goods. There were no other stalls.

Often we'd have relatives come to stay. My mother's family came from Instow, just a few miles from Barnstaple, and those who had moved away to South Wales used to like to come back. I remember my aunt from Cardiff making my mother go with her to enquire about her son, my cousin, who had been lost aboard HMS *Glorious* when it was torpedoed at Narvik in June 1940. She was desperate for good news, but there were very few survivors – only forty-three out of more than 1200 men. My aunt never got over that loss. But that was the only tragedy that struck our family: others suffered much more. We were lucky to be living where we were.

Dolly, in Maidenhead, Berkshire, also recalls life going on much as before:

I was the fifth of fifteen children and every time a new baby came along, we older girls had to look after the little ones until our mother was up and about again. I remember playing in the street with friends who lived nearby: there were no cars, so it was a perfectly safe thing to do. We all had our jobs to do at home and we had to be home for meals, but otherwise we just went outside and amused ourselves. The local beauty spot was Burnham Beeches: it's a National Nature Reserve now, but back then it was just woodland and a lake. It was only about seven miles away but we didn't go more than once a year. With no cars, very few buses, no money to spare and all those children to look after, anything like a holiday in the modern sense was out of the question.

Like many children in town and country alike, Jenny endured separation from her father. Apart from that, life in Shropshire was largely untouched:

My father had joined the RAF when he was eighteen, before the war. He was out in the Middle East for a long time, in some sort of administrative role, and he was invited to come back to the UK and train to be a pilot, but he was enjoying himself too much, so he stayed – which is probably just as well, as if he had become a pilot, he could easily have died. But he came back just before war broke out.

My parents had been due to get married the day before the war started and they had to postpone it because my father had to report for duty. They had a very quiet wedding a week or so later, then my father went off to a camp in Scotland and my mother moved back in with her parents in Oswestry, on the Welsh borders. Then just over a year later, during the Battle of Britain, she had me.

We lived in a little house, with an outside toilet and no proper bathroom, just a tin bath-tub in front of the fire. My grandfather had a big allotment as well as his garden, so he grew plenty of vegetables. He was also a churchwarden and he grew lilies and things for the church. So we were well supplied with veg and fruit. He came from farming stock in Wales and I think we probably got a few things we shouldn't have done from his relations – eggs and things like that, because my grandparents didn't keep hens. I expect we did better than many.

The only bomb I ever knew about landed in the grounds of the big estate belonging to Lord Harlech, just outside Oswestry, and made a crater. It was almost certainly dumped by a bomber on its way back from a raid on Liverpool. So that was a bit of excitement that of course I knew nothing at all about; I was far too young.

My father visited us sometimes – my brother was born

in 1944, so Dad must have come home on leave at some point. Then he went to India and didn't return till after Partition in 1947. So although he was a lovely man and we later became very close, my first real memory of him is from when I was seven. But I remember my childhood as a happy time – my grandmother was sweet, and so was my mother; my grandfather was a bit more stern, but I was his first grandchild and he absolutely loved me and spoiled me.

Brenda, aged four in 1939, spent the war years in Enham (now Enham-Alamein) in Hampshire:

It was a very close-knit place and I played with a lot of the local children. There was a farm in the village and we used to go into the fields at harvest time. To get to school, when I was really small Mum used to take me on the back of her bike, but when I was a bit older, I walked with the other children. We had to go along a path through two cornfields – about a mile and a half. We were always told, 'If the siren goes, lie down.' I won't say it happened very often, but we did sometimes hear the siren go when we were on our way to or from school and had to lie down in the cornfield until the all clear went. My standing joke for years has been that I once lay down in the cornfield with Harold Oliver. Harold was an evacuee who lived in the village and came to school with us; the siren went as we were crossing the field together. But we were only about eight, so it wasn't anything shocking.

In the summer holidays we helped out in the cornfields, stacking the sheaves of corn. We'd often be up there at nine or ten o'clock at night, because it was still light. We didn't get paid, it was just something we were expected to do. The farmer lived in the village and his cows used to come down his track and out on to the main road and leave their whatshername all over the place – the pavements always had cow dung on them. We didn't get milk in bottles in those days: one of the farmhands used to come round with the milk churn and knock on the door. You'd take your jug to the door and he'd ladle the milk in for you. Because you didn't have a fridge to put it in, you'd have a little net with beads on it that hung over the top of the jug to keep the flies out.

Two of my aunts lived near us and each had one daughter, my cousins. When the sirens went off at night we used to go to Auntie Mill's and the three of us girls, aged between about five and ten, were put into the cupboard under the stairs on a mattress. The mums would stay in the dining room and get under the table – not that I think it would have protected them very much. But we didn't have a very horrendous war – the nearest bomb I can remember was at Goodworth Clatford, about five miles away. We were lucky.

Sue, born a year after the war started, lived in a Sussex village:

We'd been in military accommodation before my father was sent to India at the end of 1940. He spent most of the war on the Northwest Frontier there. My mother, with two little girls and a third on the way, decided she needed to get a house organised and we moved to Old Farm, an Elizabethan 'yeoman's house' on the edge of Groombridge, near Tunbridge Wells, very close to where Mum's mother lived. I remember a huge chimney going up in the middle of the main downstairs room, dividing the dining room from the sitting room, which had a big open fireplace. At the side there was a small kitchen and a room which had been the dairy, but which was turned into two little bedrooms, where we children slept; there was one main bedroom upstairs, and above the sitting room was our nursery. It had open floorboards, and where they had slightly drifted apart over the years you could see right through into the room below. When the weather was bad, that's where we played, but when the weather was not so awful, we would be outside, immediately.

Mum cultivated a veg patch, so that she could grow her own vegetables, and we had a shelter in the garden – all you saw of it was the hole that you went into. Inside it was lined with bricks. We played in it sometimes, but it was cold and damp and very dark, so it wasn't an ideal place for playing in. It did have frogs in it, though, which we found quite interesting.

Beyond the garden we were surrounded by a farm. There were crops and cattle, but we three girls used to go on 'picnics' in the cornfields. I can't imagine what we took for food, but they had broken biscuits in the grocer's, so that might be what we had. Certainly, nothing very much. We would go and play in the fields once the harvest had been done – there were no combine harvesters or anything like that, of course, but they would have built the stooks of corn up, ready to be threshed. We used to take my mother's teddy bear with us. He was about three feet tall – about the same size as us – and on one particular occasion we came back without him.

The first thing my mother said when she saw us was, 'Where's Teddy?'

We were horrified. We'd been playing hide and seek in the cornfield – it was absolutely our favourite game – so we said, 'He must be hiding in the corn stooks.' My mother came with us and we looked in every single stook in that field and could we find Teddy? No. We must have left him lying there and the farmer or somebody must have come and picked him up, but it was such a small village, if they had done, you'd have thought somebody locally would have known. He was never found. Mum was furious, of course, and very upset, because he was her teddy from when she was a little girl.

That wasn't the only crisis we had in the fields. We had a village girl, Elsie, who came to look after us when Mum was cooking or digging in the garden or whatever and one day she took us out for a proper picnic in the field. She was giving me a piggyback at the bottom of the field when the cows came in. She was so scared that she dropped me on the ground and ran shrieking back to my mother.

Mum looked at her and said, 'Where are the girls?' and she had to say, 'Oh, they're still in the field', where the cows were happily lumbering about, taking no notice of us at all. But I had actually broken my leg in the fall – well, I'd cracked it, what they call a greenstick fracture, and I couldn't walk.

Poor Elsie – she didn't last very long after that.

There was another drama that arose from hide and seek. I was hiding in a ditch and found that I was sitting on an ant heap. Of course I couldn't get up and run away, because I'd have been seen. I remember crouching there, knowing that I was being bitten and thinking, 'I can't move. They'll see me if I move.' I had to stay there until I was found and I had a lot of ant bites by then. I was wearing a skirt – we always did, so if we were doing roly-polys or head stands we just tucked our skirts into our knickers. Anyway, on this occasion the ants got everywhere. I went home and Mum stuck me in a cold bath and covered me with calamine lotion to relieve the itching. It put me off hide and seek for a little while.

Picnics further away than the field at the bottom of the garden were an occasional summer treat. Sue continues:

My mother had a friend who loved horses and had two boys about our age. She had two ponies for the boys, the larger of which pulled a pony trap, and she used to do all her shopping and all her running around in the trap, because no one had cars, of course. Actually, we did have a car, but it was up on blocks for the entire duration of the war and there certainly wouldn't have been any petrol to put in it.

Anyway, on one occasion this friend took us in the trap up on to Ashdown Forest. I don't remember much about the picnic, except that it was fun to play hide and seek in the bracken. We would have had paste in our sandwiches – meat paste or fish paste, you could get both, but that was about the only thing we did have in sandwiches. Sometimes bridge rolls, sometimes bread. The village was well supplied; it had a baker, a butcher (which had a small cattle market behind it, where the meat came from), a grocer, a post office and a doctor.

Joyce in Suffolk also has fond memories of picnics:

One treat for a picnic by the river was cucumber sandwiches: my mother grew ridge cucumbers and they had a lot more flavour than the ones you could buy. I absolutely loved cucumber sandwiches. A lot of people used to go down and picnic by the river and I can still see the oak tree that was the best spot – you wanted to get there early in case someone else got there first and sat under it.

Evelyn, living in Kendal in the Lake District, wrote to her husband Ernest, serving overseas, about taking their two small children, Michael and Jeanne, on a picnic with friends:

On Sunday, Florry and I took the 'cherubs' and Joan picnic-ing. How I wish you could have seen the pleasure Michael derived from 'getting-off' alone. He packed the tin-opener into a bag – 'Yes!' I said. 'Just like your daddy. Nothing without the tin opener.' 'Can I fetch a bottle of lemonade, Mummy? Wait for me, Shoan (Joan). I won't be long,' and off we set, the three of them with a bottle of lemonade under their arm. Up the 'A' road we went, and had tea made at the farm on top of the second hill (thinking it would be easier to carry if we took an early tea), and then we discovered a very attractive lane turning off to the left, and went to explore. What beauty! Ernest, I never dreamt of such beauty so near at hand. To our right, the wood rose uphill, shading a mass of bluebells and primroses and, to our left, the woodland sloped downwards, into the rushing, splashing river. Keeping to the pathway, we swung left, coming along the bank of the river and into a village. You know the one. Out again onto the main road by the bridge you and I so often travelled, and home to tea. The cherubs in bed and a cigarette by the fire.

Living in a remote place meant that even going to school could be an adventure. Sue again:

We went to what they called a 'dame school' in Langton, two and a half miles away up a steep hill. It would have been all right coming home on a bike, but not so good going up. So we went by bus – the number 91. It went every half an hour. We had strict instructions not to talk to strangers, but everyone on the bus knew us and the bus drivers knew us, so we were perfectly safe. Mum would see us on to the bus and we'd be dropped off in Langton village.

Miss Bird had only just started her school – my older sister Margaret was one of her first pupils. There were never more than about twenty-six pupils, and at the beginning there might have been fifteen or sixteen, with only three or four of them older than Margaret. Miss Bird had hired an old garage with a side area that acted as our cloakroom. There was a separate room for the 'transition' class, which you moved up to after kindergarten, and then she'd divided the main hall into two with a curtain to make two classes for the older and younger children. She took boys till they were eight, when they went off to prep school, and girls till eleven, when they would either go on to boarding school or to the local high school in Tunbridge Wells. We had lunch in the village – we went down the road to Anne's Pantry for lunch, a little café that did midday meals. So right from the start, aged only three or four, we did a full day. We had a rest after lunch – we had to lie down on the floor – but we were there all day.

Sylvia in rural Norfolk also remembers a trek to school:

It was a long bus ride, because the nearest secondary school was in King's Lynn, about thirteen miles away.

We had to catch the bus at eight o'clock in the morning. The road we lived in was off the main road, so we could see the bus coming. In those days the bus drivers used to know who was supposed to get on the bus at which stops and they would look down the road and wait if they could see you running towards them. It was quite a friendly arrangement, except that once the war started, the bus dropped from being one an hour to one every two hours – so you had to catch the bus, whatever else; otherwise you were in dead trouble because you couldn't get to school. And the two hours was a bit of a nuisance, because it made you very late if you missed the bus on the way home.

We couldn't play on the beach at Heacham during the war, because it was barbed wired off, but there was a lot of open land behind the beaches and we did play there. I remember picking rosehips and the Women's Institute making rosehip jelly in the school kitchens. There were lots of hedgerows around and a lot of wild roses.

We used to have hens, and if you had hens you didn't get an egg ration; you got food for the hens instead and if you only had a few, you got to keep the eggs. If you had a lot of hens, I think you had to put the eggs into the general system – it would have been controlled in some way – but as an ordinary household we weren't affected by that. My father had also seen fit to buy some rabbits, so that we would always have rabbit to eat. But he made the mistake of buying white ones with little black spots and we never ate one. Friends and neighbours did – we passed them on – but we wouldn't eat them; they had become our pets.

Apart from rationing, most people in the village really knew very little about the war. We were slightly different, because my sister lost her husband. She had joined the WAAF [Women's Auxillary Air Force] as a volunteer, and in about 1941, she married an airman who was shot down and killed only six months later. I didn't understand then as much as I did later on, of course, but I remember what she was like and how awful it was. We also had a neighbour in Heacham who was in the RAF, like my father, and he was killed very early on in the war, at the base at Bircham Newton. He was taking a bomb apart and it blew up. So I was quite close to the action in that respect.

For many children from the cities and suburbs, war brought a first taste of country life. David describes the contrast between Beckenham and Devon as…

…like going from Hell to Heaven really. When you went for a walk there were flowers – I remember irises in particular – and elderberries, which we squeezed like wine into our mouths. Everything seemed green, perfect, peaceful and there was probably slightly more food around.

But it wasn't all sweetness. On about the second day we were there my mother sent me up the road to buy tomatoes from someone who had glasshouses. It was only about eight hundred yards away, so my little sister and I went up, got the tomatoes and were on our way back again across the fields when a group of eight boys ambushed us. They didn't attack my sister but, as an evacuee, I was a target for them and they all set on me. I managed to say, 'This isn't fair. I'll fight one of you.' They picked the oldest boy – I was ten, he was at least twelve. But as the son of an agricultural labourer, he was from a poor family, undernourished, I suppose, and not very well developed. I managed to hold my own. I'd sent my sister home with the tomatoes and I was winning the fight when she came back with our mother to rescue me.

My mother kept asking me what had happened and was I all right, but I didn't want to talk. I wanted to keep my face turned away from the other boys, because I knew I was going to cry at any moment. And I did eventually allow that out. But the fact is, looking at it from their point of view, some of them had lost their dad at Dunkirk and they knew that official evacuees from London were mollycoddled. I knew one boy who'd had a lovely jacket and shoes sent over from Canada. So they were contrasting their poverty with the easy time they thought the evacuees had – they didn't know that I wasn't from London and wasn't an official evacuee, so I had none of these privileges.

I did eventually make friends – not with the boy I'd been fighting, because he was a bit older, but with the others, who were my age. One of them was the farmer's son and I learned to help him with jobs round the farm, bringing the cows in, and, later in the year, digging up vegetables and all sorts of things. The farmer was reasonably well off, whereas I learned later that some of the labourers were only getting ten shillings a week – that's 50p. This was at a time when the average pay in London might have been about three pounds. If you were a manager in an office you might get five pounds. But in Devon there was poverty.

There was also a certain amount of sadness. There were plenty of widows from the First World War, including one old lady who would jump out in front of a convoy of artillery every time they went through the village. Her son had gone missing during the first war and all those years later, she'd still look into the back of the lorries to see if 'her Charlie' was there.

Shirley lived not far from David, on the fringes of London and Kent:

My grandmother was in Petersfield, which was near enough to Portsmouth to be dangerous, so at the very start of the war, when invasion was expected any day, she got a map and a pin and she put the pin in where she thought it would take Hitler longest to get to. That's how we ended up in Hereford. She bought a house and took us four children there with her. My grandmother was about sixty and my grandfather was sixty-five and retired, so they had this house full of their grandchildren. In addition to us there was my grandmother's other daughter, who was a semi-invalid, and her husband, who was much older, about the same age as my grandfather. I think there was another child – there were nine of us altogether – and the local billeting officer came round and said, 'This house can take sixteen.' So my grandmother took in a whole lot more people, including her youngest sister's three children; we children were all put in the attic, in a row of iron beds, which I suppose the billeting officer supplied.

In the summer my grandmother rented a cottage in the country and took us children there – we went in 1940, 1941 and 1942. We went at Easter, too, but not at Christmas because it was too cold. It was in a little village called Bircher Common, quite close to where we were living in Hereford. There was no water or electricity or anything. We were at the top of a hill; at the bottom, a quarter of a mile away, there was a well, where we had to go to get water. The woman in charge of the well was called Mad Nell; she had a sort of contorted face and wore red spotted handkerchiefs from Woolworths round her neck. She used to charge a farthing a bucket for water. When she had enough money, she would walk into Leominster, which was five miles away, and buy another red spotted handkerchief from Woolworths.

That cottage is where I did my first cooking. My grandmother cooked on the fire, with a triangular metal stand to put a cauldron or kettle on. One time she sprained her ankle and was in bed upstairs. My grandfather was away for the day for some reason, but before he went, he had shot a rabbit and that was to be our dinner. So my grandmother called down from the bedroom, telling me how to cook it: I had to skin it and gut it and everything, then boil it, keep the water and throw some vegetables in. I remember also starting to write my first book, which was *100 Ways to Cook the Common Apple*, because in that part of the world we were surrounded by cider orchards.

The lavatory was right at the end of the garden; one summer, it had a wasps' nest in it and we all got constipated, because nobody wanted to go and sit there and be exposed to the wasps.

There wasn't much bombing in Herefordshire, but a German fighter plane once came down on the common in front of us. We weren't allowed to go and see it, but the boys of the village did. I don't know what happened to the pilot, but it showed that we weren't necessarily safe where Grandmother had put the pin.

We never saw my father during this time, but my mother used to visit occasionally, travelling by train. Trains were always very full, people in the corridors and sometimes soldiers lying in the upper bits, which were supposed to be for luggage. If German planes came over, the train stopped and all the lights went out. Then, when the all clear came, it could carry on – until the next threat. You can do London to Hereford in three hours now, but once it took Mum nearly twenty-four hours, standing up all the way. She was always absolutely exhausted when she reached us.

There was another interesting feature to life in Hereford, as Shirley continues. As with Maggie in Barry, American soldiers were the first black people she had ever seen:

> Although we didn't know it at the time, this was where the commandos were trained. The black American soldiers were extremely popular. They could dance very well, among other things. The US army was segregated, so if they went into a pub the white men didn't want the black men going into the saloon parlour with them. They complained to the landlords, and the landlords said, 'We *like* the chocolate soldiers. If you don't want to drink with them, you can stay away.'

Mervyn was brought up on a farm in Gloucestershire, but that wasn't immune from bombing, either:

> Our first taste of the war at first hand occurred a couple of months after the Dunkirk evacuation. It was 3 August 1940. The previous evening, we had finished haymaking in the field furthest from the house and had sat round the hayrick for a late tea/early supper before returning to the farm to milk the twenty or so cows which provided the main income at that time. A neighbour remarked that it was so quiet, it was impossible to believe there was a war.
>
> Twenty-four hours or so later, we had just gone to bed when there was the whistle and roar of exploding bombs. They sounded quite near. After breakfast the

following morning I was sent to see where they had fallen and found a crater exactly where we had been sitting the evening before. What had happened was that a German bomber had jettisoned his load after either being chased by a fighter or being unable to reach his target. There were eight bombs in total. Six had fallen harmlessly in Westridge Woods, with the final two in our field. Casualties I found nearby were a rabbit and a mouse.

The craters were about five to six feet across and about eighteen inches deep – not large by the standards of what were dropped later in the war, but equally lethal. As word got around, we had many visitors who wanted to see the craters and to find a piece of shrapnel. We boys made a bob or two by selling what we had found. A fortnight or so later, a farmer arrived and begged us for some shrapnel. Seeing my father at market some weeks later, he said he need not have bothered – he had had nine bombs on his own land that night.

Bristol became a major target. We could see the anti-aircraft fire exploding in the sky over the city and the glare of the fires and hear the bombs as they exploded. We couldn't see Bristol itself as Westridge Hill lay in the way. At school, if there was a daylight raid we marched to a sunken lane shielded by trees and there we remained until the all clear sounded. On one occasion that was very late in the afternoon, when the British Aeroplane Company factory at Filton was the target, I got home too late to share my part of the milking, so was not popular with my father or brother for giving them extra work.

Jim, aged eleven, was evacuated from South London to Northiam in East Sussex, where he lived very happily in the home of Mr and Mrs Skinner, the village milkman and his wife, and had his first experience of picking hops:

We were up early next morning, where it became obvious that Mrs Skinner was no stranger to the annual three weeks spent in the hop fields. Flasks of tea were filled and sandwiches made ready for the walk to Farrant's Farm. There were between fifteen and twenty families assembled for their allocation of a bin. I just believe it was called a bin, although it was made of sacking; they measured about five feet long and two feet deep. Being semi-detached, each family had a close neighbour, making village gossip a part of the hopping experience. A framework of fashioned pine trunks used year after year supported the deep sack trough. Our immediate neighbours were a married couple who could pick hops nearly as fast as a machine. He must have been out of work for he was always there, and they usually had plenty of friends to help boost their pickings. When it came to measuring and collection time, our neighbour's bin usually contained twice as many hops as ours. I didn't work at the bin because, by mutual agreement, I was best sitting on the ground, filling my own basket. Near emptying time, Mrs Skinner carried out a quality control inspection to ensure that there were no leaves in my contribution.

Mrs Skinner did allow me to take a break for exercise. On reflection, my time off just preceding lunch may have been a well-calculated ploy, ensuring a punctual return. I never found any washing facilities, but that's how it was in those days. Picking hops made your hands blacker than I had ever seen before, so at picnic time, that meant some sort of protection. Out would come the tissue paper, followed by sandwiches and a nice cup of tea. What I forgot whilst describing the early morning packing of our picnic was the fruit, always apples and pears that were in plentiful supply. Most villagers had a tree or two and many had a mini orchard.

Sheila, another Londoner, had had hop-picking 'holidays' with her family before the war. Those three weeks in Kent in late August and early September continued throughout the hostilities:

My mother was a cook in a school, so she could have time off in the holidays. My dad was a builder, so he was perhaps doing one job one week and another job the next. It wasn't easy for him to go away for any length of time. So he would get my mum, my brother and me down to the station and leave us. We lived in the East End of London and we walked to London Bridge to catch a train down into Kent.

My father would come with us to the station, pushing

this thing that he'd made that he called a cart, but was really like a half-sized coffin on wheels with all our stuff in. The farm we went to probably had about eight or nine families, and each family had its own little wooden hut. The farmer provided straw for the bedding, but we'd bring our own mattress covers and stuff the straw into them to make the beds. Mum used to take a pair of curtains to separate off the bedroom section – you could take all sorts of things to make the hut like a miniature home. We took a bucket and a bowl, saucepans, plates, cutlery, all the sort of things you'd need to live in the hut. We'd take some food with us, too, tinned stuff like corned beef or stewed steak, and then at the weekends we'd do our shopping with our ration books in the local village or town, to stock up for the week.

Anyway, Dad would wheel this cart on to the luggage part of the train. At the other end, the local farmer sent a lorry to meet all the pickers – there were lots of us on the same train – and pick up their little wagons or prams, or whatever they had their stuff in. It would all be piled into the lorry and we'd be driven to the farm. Then we'd be allocated a hut.

Although it was a holiday for us it was a working holiday for the parents: they would pick the hops and we children would muck in for a while, then we'd go off and play. They used to start very early in the morning and work till three or four in the afternoon, then go home and cook a meal. Mum would have a fire going and we'd have a big pot hanging over it on a hook and she'd make a lovely stew.

And of course the farmer had lovely produce, which didn't cost you anything – you could get plenty of vegetables from him. We really enjoyed our meals out there. In the evenings we'd all congregate, sit round the fires and sing songs, things like that.

When you went to the start of the 'pick', as they called it, you drove into the field and it was beautiful – a lovely lush green, with new leaves. It was like walking into a church full of greenery, and the smell of the hops was not a perfume, exactly, but a really beautiful, refreshing sort of smell. Hop picking isn't difficult work and it was very pleasant, really. You had a big canvas bin with a thick wooden frame, like a bed frame, and you could sit on the side of it while you were throwing the hops into the bin. It was quite comfortable. The hops grew on wires that had to be pulled down so that you could reach them over your head. You'd pull the bine down, pull the dark leaves off and throw them away, then scoop the hops themselves into the bin. About twice a day a man used to come round with what they called a 'bushel basket'. It was quite a big basket; when it was three-quarters full that was a bushel – a bit more than a cubic foot – and you got paid by the bushel. The man would write it down in a book and it would mount up over the three weeks, so at the end you'd have this lovely large sum of money. In the meantime, if you were short of money for your shopping, you could go to the farmer and show him your book and he'd advance you what you needed out of your earnings. So you didn't starve.

Right: A three-year-old tries out the harvesting machine. July 1943.

Left: Schoolboys tend to a flock of sheep at Ashwell Village School, Hertfordshire.

Right: Young Londoners improvise a cricket pitch in front of their blitzed homes in Canning Town.

Summer 1939: the National Fire
Service takes over Primrose Hill
School in London and run drills in
the playground.

© John Tiranti

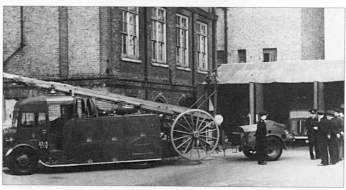

Left: A blacksmith's mother takes over the forge while her son is away fighting. She is seen here forging chains for the Navy – hot work in the thick of summer.

© *Mirrorpix*

Right: 'A perfect picture of life during the war.' Bridget in her home-made knitted dress admires baby brother Martin; mother Marjorie wears a scarf wound into a turban in imitation of Clementine Churchill; and the backdrop is the family's Anderson shelter. © *Bridget Clarke*

Below: London's 'blitzed babies' enjoying the tranquillity of seaside air at a West Country resort. © *Mirrorpix*

Summer sports: American soldiers playing baseball amid the ruins in Liverpool (above) and Canadian Army and US Air Force in a game at the Hounslow Cricket Ground (below).

Above: American soldiers try their hand at the Maypole with children at the Spring Festival at Hindhead. June 1942.

Right: 'Wartime Summer': a sailor lends a hand when a holidaymaker becomes entangled in barbed wire.

Left: The first black female Red Cross workers to arrive in Britain, pictured taking a walk with two black GIs in Bristol.

Right: Members of the Women's Auxiliary Territorial Services learn about motorcycling from soldiers at a Manchester barracks. Late summer 1942.

Left: Three NAAFI girls adjust their watches by the clock tower in Calais.

Left: Boys in post-war Berlin are served a ration of gruel in their school playground. The rations are provided by the British authorities. Summer 1945.

© *Keystone/Getty Images*

Right : Queuing to buy oranges and bananas at a stall in bomb-wrecked London in 1940. A sign on the stall reads: 'Hitler's bombs can't beat us. Our oranges came through Musso's Lake' [service slang for the Mediterranean].

© *Keystone/Getty Images*

Left: Damaged buildings in Cannon Street in the City of London during the Blitz. May 1941.

© *Central Press/Getty Images*

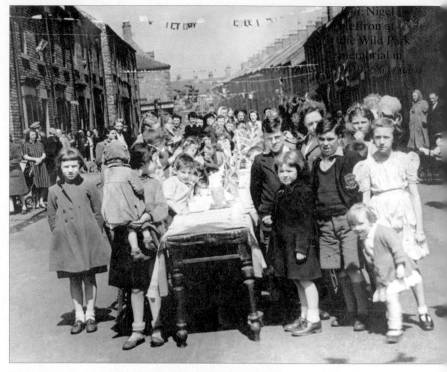

Above: VE Day celebrations and 'Victory Tea' in North Shields. Children were supplied with chocolate, sweets and oranges. 8 May 1945.   © NCJ Archive/Mirrorpix

Below left: Post-war celebrations in Torquay.   © Mirrorpix

Below right: Dancing in the street on VE Day in Piccadilly Gardens, Manchester.   © Manchester Evening News Archive/Mirrorpix

I know all this because we carried on hop picking after the war, when I was old enough to take it all in. But I remember one occasion during the war quite clearly. I was only tiny, perhaps five, and I was in a field with Mum. There were a Spitfire and a German plane literally firing at each other, just above our heads. We were standing there looking up, watching, and we saw the German plane coming down with its tail alight. Suddenly everyone was running and shouting, 'Quick, quick, quick!' My mother threw me down into the bin, with all the hops, and she ran off the field. We waited until the noise had stopped. What must have happened was that the German, realising he had been hit, thought, 'Right, I'm going, I'll take some of that lot with me', so he was machine-gunning into the field while he could, just shooting at the hop pickers.

They did that sort of thing during the war. My husband was evacuated to Essex and he was on a train at night with his mum and four brothers, heading away from London: it was fired at by planes that were coming in to raid.

On a happier note, I remember some young students who were studying to go into the church; they used to come round the hop huts on a Sunday afternoon and have a sing-song round the fire – sometimes we'd sing hymns, but there were boy scout songs, too, like 'There were birds, birds, singing in the trees, in the trees…' They were really lovely evenings. It was a very happy three weeks of our lives. And at the end you got a lovely lump sum of money, which meant we all got treated – new clothes and other things that we couldn't have afforded otherwise.

Valerie, whose parents had a farm in southwest Scotland, remembers the summer jobs:

Hay-cutting in June was a busy time and it was 'all hands on deck', with men cutting hay with a reaper then building onto pikes which were then taken to the farmyard one at a time on a bogie cart then built into stacks. This was feed for the cattle in winter. I remember Mother baking to feed the workers, usually large soda scones; we children would carry baskets of baking and cans of milk to the field for the men at break times. The highlight was getting a lift back on the bogie.

John had been evacuated from London to a home in the country, between Maidenhead and Windsor:

It was an elderly couple, Mr and Mrs Higgins, with three daughters, and they already had two evacuees from London – two more girls – when they took me in. The old man used to drink a lot and we kept out of his way when that happened, so I spent a lot of time on the farm next door, which was owned by a man named Churchill. No relation to Winston, so far as I know. I got very involved with the various tasks. I don't know what the girls did while I was doing that; perhaps working on the farm was seen as a boy's job, because I don't remember the girls being involved. I was friendly with the farmer's daughter, Enid, though. Her father had a Morris 8 under cover in one of the barns and she and I used to sit in it and pretend we were driving round in it.

When I first went there the farm had a carthorse; later, they got a tractor. I remember the horse was used for ploughing in the first year I was there; then when they got the tractor, they used that for ploughing and kept the horse just to pull the cart.

I used to help with the corn and the hay – those were big summer jobs – and after that, there was the gleaning. When they cut the corn there was an awful lot of waste; we used to go round the field with sacks, and probably off a ten-acre field we'd get three big sacks of ears of corn, which we kept to feed the chickens with. Today you wouldn't get any corn at all – you'd just get bales of straw.

Although there was lots of hay and corn it was really a dairy farm: there were about forty cows and they were all hand-milked, there were no machines then. You'd just sit on those little stools and get on with it.

I helped with the muck-spreading, too. They used to take the muck and make heaps and I would help spread it round a particular patch: no mechanical muck-spreaders in the 1940s.

Farming was hard work in those days. Today, a man goes round with a big machine and harvests a whole field of corn, and threshes it and takes the grain out, and another comes along with a trailer and collects it, and drops the straw, and then another goes along and bales it up. They're doing in a day the work that ten men would probably have taken three or four days to do. Same with hedging – where I live now, we've got several acres of land with about 400 yards of hedge; we pay a man fifty quid and he goes along and does the whole thing in a couple of hours. It was a different world during the war.

Living in the country brought other tasks, too. John continues:

Another of my jobs was to go down to the farmyard to get milk every day. The fresh milk would be poured into a container, then run down a cooler, which looked like a washboard, and into a churn. Then they'd dip a stainless-steel ladle into it and fill up the container I'd brought. It wasn't pasteurised, of course, and it had a lot of cream in it. When I got home to London and saw the milk we got there, I asked my mother, 'Where's all the cream?' By the time the dairy had messed about and skimmed all the cream off, there wasn't a lot left, it seemed to me. So that was quite funny – I wasn't impressed by London milk.

On Saturdays I had yet another job. I used to go over to another local farm, where they had cows and pigs. I was friendly with the daughter, Daphne. She was a bit older than me and we used to take out the pony and trap and go down to Bray, to the hotels there, and get all the swill, which we'd bring back and cook up for the pigs. I don't suppose you'd be allowed to do it today. But the amount of cutlery we found in there, you wouldn't believe – it had just been thrown out with the scraps.

As for the war, John recalls:

We were aware of it in the sense that we listened to the radio and knew what was going on, but it was distant. One German bomber was shot down and landed in a field on the Windsor–Maidenhead road; I don't know how true this is, but it was said that by the time the authorities got there a lot of the Perspex had gone, because the local people used it to make jewellery: they took what they thought would be useful. And I remember one bomb about five miles away, but apart from that, the war didn't really affect us as such.

Obviously, lots of things were rationed, but in the country there was plenty of bartering going on for eggs and bacon and so on. We were better off than people in the town. Mr Higgins grew vegetables – he had a big veg garden and every year he'd dig a trench, then he'd borrow a cart from the local wealthy family, who had horses, and he'd gather up manure from there. He'd fill the trench and work manure into the whole bed, so we would have veg all the time, beautiful veg. He worked hard at that. So we were never short of veg, never short of eggs, but things like toilet paper you couldn't get – it was sheets of newspaper on a string in the outside loo: you had to be really desperate to go out there.

It was a typical country house – well, there was a row of about ten of them – but they all had two buildings outside, one was the loo and the other was the coal house. But they kept all sorts of things apart from coal in there; in the house they had a little bathroom and they kept the coal in the bath – for what reason, I'm not really sure. Perhaps it was just the biggest receptacle they had. We had a big tin bath and Friday night was bath night. Us kids went in last – it was like mud by the time we got into that water.

But really, the shortages were of luxury things – sweets, chocolate, soap; with basic things, you got your rations and with so many of us in the house, we combined to get decent quantities.

It was a happy time, when the weather was good. When I got back to school in London, we had to write an essay that was something to do with where we'd been evacuated, so I did the seasons of the year on the farm. When I handed it in, I was accused of taking it out of a book and I explained that I'd lived like that for five years, so I knew it by heart.

Maggie also remembers the effort that went into feeding the pigs:

I had a great-aunt, Aunty Till, and she and Uncle George had a smallholding about ten miles outside Cardiff. She would come in with her horse and cart with a few bins in the cart, and collect the contents of the 'pig bucket' from various customers. People would put potato peelings and any food scraps into this bucket and leave it out in the lane; once a week, Aunty Till would come and tip the contents of the buckets into her bins and take them home. Then Uncle George would boil it all up and feed it to the pigs. There was no extra dry food – this swill was all the pigs got.

We went out there a couple of times on the bus and I remember Uncle George used to kill a pig now and again and slice it up and hang the bits up to dry on hooks in the kitchen ceiling. Then I think he used to smoke it. But I can see him sitting in the kitchen with a cup of tea, which he'd always pour into his saucer. So he'd be holding the saucer of tea with two hands and sticking both little fingers out in that supposedly elegant way, then slurping the tea really noisily. With bits of pig carcass hanging all around him.

Pig bins weren't an exclusively rural amenity, as Bridget recalls from Wembley Park:

The pig bins were quite complicated because you couldn't put in anything that was really edible: if you put in half a loaf that was stale you might be arrested or certainly told off for wasting food – you should have turned it into breadcrumbs or something. It was only potato peelings and apple cores and things like that that you were allowed to throw away.

Deidre was living with her mother and grandparents in Llangattock, in the Brecon Beacons, and remembers an unpleasant feature of village life:

We didn't have a sewerage scheme in the village. It had been due to be put in, but what with the war and the cost, it was abandoned and I don't think we had sewerage until 1955.

Once a week, always on a Friday night, a big cart used to come round, drawn by two horses. It was sometimes called the Tumbler, but we always called it the Honey Cart. I have no idea why – it must been a joke, because it wasn't exactly sweet-smelling. There were two men and they'd stop at various points round the village. I remember them stopping in front of our shop, because there were two lanes with little houses in that area, and then they'd go to the main body of the village as well. So they would pull up and go down to the toilet, which in my grandparents' case was down the lane a little way, and they would take away the full bucket, empty it and put it back again. Then they'd take whatever they'd collected down to a local farm and it would be spread on the fields there, I believe. Certainly, the mushrooms were amazing.

So, consequently, nothing happened in the village on a Friday night. If they wanted to have a harvest thanksgiving, which in those days would have been in the summer, rather than in the autumn as it often is now, it couldn't be on a Friday, because as you can imagine, it wasn't very nice. Everybody kept indoors.

The collection was supposed to be done after dark, but of course in summer if they hadn't started until it got dark, they'd never have got it done. It was quite a big village, so it took a few hours.

Charlotte had a more glamorous introduction to country living:

My father had been in the RAF, but then he joined a branch of the SOE – the Special Operations Executive. He helped to set up a unit on the edge of Woburn Park in Bedfordshire, so for the rest of the war we lived near there, occupying the whole of the top floor of Toddington Manor House. I assume it had been requisitioned. It was very old, but had been altered considerably. It had stable blocks and a dairy and massive grounds with a couple of lakes, and a long, long drive, the end of which was very much uphill to get on to the main road. So my mother would have done that trip, on her bicycle, quite often, to get to the shops and any time she needed to go anywhere. It's a stop on the M1 now, but it was out in the country then.

I can remember a fete being held in the grounds of the manor and I think my father helped to make a big figure, like a guy, of Hitler – you threw things at it and won a prize.

Jeanne's father had an industrial job, but her family had a holiday refuge in the country:

He was a mechanical engineer, working for ICI in Billingham-on-Tees, where I was born. It was bombed early in the war and he was moved to Heysham, near Lancaster, where there was another ICI factory, making petrol. So we all moved from the east coast to the west coast. My father was in charge of the factory, which resulted in our acquiring a telephone. A great excitement. I used to come back from school and ask, 'Has it rung?' Of course it hadn't, but it was for emergencies in case he had suddenly to go in.

During the summer holidays we went up to a farm outside Lancaster and stayed in a stationary caravan that my father had done up: he'd bought a shell of a caravan and made it into a place where four people could live and sleep. It wasn't a matter of getting away from bombing, just doing something for the holidays. It was our main escape from daily life. My father cycled to work in Heysham every day. I still have a tiny Pepys diary that I kept in 1943 and it says, 'Tidied van' nearly every day while we were there. It had berths on either side and a table in the middle; how we cooked or anything, I can't remember. But there is one entry that says 'Tidied van. Did potatoes', so we obviously did cook. And I've noted things like 'Dinner – fried fish. Yum!' Meat was hard to come by, but we must have got fish from Morecambe Bay, which was quite nearby. The farmer's wife used to cook for us, too: I remember her making delicious egg custards, but my diary also has the surprising entry, 'Supper at farm. Chips – ugh!' We picked blackberries and, according to my diary, dandelions, but whether we ate the leaves in salads or my mother made them into a drink, I don't remember.

I was still at the 'going out to play in the fields' stage,

but my brother and I did help with the haymaking. We also built corn bales on top of a wagon that was pulled by a tractor. I was allowed to drive the tractor on the farm at age twelve. You just let off the brake and it went!

Martin, also working in the fields, came quite close to hostilities:

One summer holiday, I volunteered for work on a farm near to Harpenden. Most the time was spent gathering sheaves of wheat or barley into stooks of about eight sheaves, stood leaning against each other to dry in the airflow between them. On other occasions I was allowed to drive a horse and cart down the lane to the field, but on one occasion I cut the corner too fine with the result that a rear wooden wheel of the cart slightly damaged a gate post. One day a battle between our fighters and a German bomber was clearly visible high above us. This was followed by the sudden appearance of a Dornier bomber flying very low over our heads and being chased by a Spitfire. The Jerry crashed in the next field, causing a great cheer from all around. What I was paid for my work I do not recall, but the weather was good and it was for 'the war effort'.

Joyce in Suffolk has her own memories of harvest time:

When they were cutting the corn, they used to give us children sticks and send us into the field to kill rabbits, even when we were very small. You could tell if there was a rabbit about by watching the top of the corn – it would weave back and forth as the rabbit ran through it. I must have had ankle socks on, because I can still feel how the stubble used to tear my ankles to pieces. I remember being in the fields with a stick, but I don't think I ever killed a rabbit.

They'd leave the corn out to dry for as long as they could and just hope it didn't rain. Oats were the first thing they cut, though – I was born in August and my father, in his broad Suffolk accent, used to call it 'oot-cuttin' time'.

Joyce's brother John remembers war interfering with one amusement:

We used to go down to the river – the Deben – to play a lot, but towards the end of the war they stopped us doing that because it was full of imitation boats and things – decoys, I suppose you'd call them – covered in canvas. The idea must have been that the Germans would be fooled into bombing them rather than anything more important further inland.

For Mervyn, summertime simply meant extra work:

Wartime summers were memorable to me mainly due to the double summertime which was introduced. It did not get dark until almost 11 p.m. and as summer meant haymaking (most of the work was by hand), it meant being out in the fields until it was almost dark and then home to milking. So very long days, both at weekends and on schooldays. My parents never kept me at home during term time, but other farmers' sons were on occasion taken out of school to help with the chores.

Double summer time was a factor in Sam's childhood experiences, too. He was born in London to a mother who was a Londoner and a father who came from the Shetland Isles. As a small boy, he and his mother undertook a particularly adventurous journey:

I was taken to Shetland twice in the wartime – the first time was in 1940, which I don't remember because I was not much more than a babe in arms, but I know it was in order to show me to my father's parents. But I do remember being taken in the summer of 1943, by which time I was nearly five. It involved catching an overnight train from London to Aberdeen and I can see us now, getting out in a darkened station with all the steam blowing around – it was very dramatic. And then going to Dyce Airport in Aberdeen to catch the first aircraft of the trip, which was very special for the time because, since it had to fly over some rather sensitive areas, all the windows had been painted black. We couldn't see out at all.

The aircraft were de Havilland Dragon Rapides – DH.89s, biplanes that probably took about eight passengers and looked as though they were held together with string. It was a tortuous journey, from Aberdeen to Inverness Dalcross, from Inverness to Wick, from Wick across the Pentland Firth to Kirkwall, and from Kirkwall to Shetland, to Sumburgh Head at the southern end of the islands. That was quite an expedition. In fact, it was a very ramshackle set-up – we weren't always on the same plane, so there was a lot of hanging about, waiting for the flight to arrive to take us on to the next stage. The planes were local services, probably mail services.

There was just my mother and me on this journey – my father was in the fire service, so he had to stay behind in London and work. It was a brave thing for my mother to do, to take me on this visit, because as I said it was terribly difficult to get there and it wasn't her family we were visiting, it was my father's, and she couldn't have known them very well. It wasn't that she was evacuating me from London, either – the whole trip was definitely just to visit the relatives.

I wonder now, too, how we got permission to do it and I think it might have had something to do with my Shetland grandfather. He had been awarded an OBE for his work with the post office – he was central to bringing radio transmission to the Shetland Isles, on behalf of the post office. It was because of this that my mother was sent, for her confinement with me, her first child, to a rather posh nursing home in Hampstead. It was really for officers' wives, but my grandfather's OBE was considered to be a notable achievement for the family and consequently I was born there instead of at the local hospital. So that OBE may have pulled a few strings for us to be permitted to travel to Shetland, too.

I remember being very excited by the harbour area in Lerwick. In those days Lerwick was a very busy port because there was a gigantic herring fleet. The herring have since disappeared and the fleet has disappeared with them, but in part of the harbour there were jetties along which I was walked as a small boy. Tight up alongside the wall of the jetties there were submarines with teeth – pointy ones, like sharks' teeth – painted on the bows and on the sides, to indicate that they were killers.

I also remember being taken further north to the great bay of Sullom Voe. We stood on the shore there and looked north to where the ocean enters the bay. There were perhaps a dozen Short Sunderland flying boats. They were a fine sight, because they were paler – whiter – than any of the other vessels I'd seen.

I went up to Shetland again recently, more than seventy years later. In the 1940s, Sullom Voe would have been very, very busy with personnel and all sorts of administration. Today, you drive along the road towards the bay and beside the road, still in existence, are the concrete bases of all the buildings there used to be. Every other aspect of those buildings has disappeared completely, but the bases, the footprint, are still there. You can still see that this was once a very busy place indeed.

We must have been in Shetland for several months during the war – I know I went to school for a while, long enough to pick up a slight accent that was soon knocked out of me once I was back in London. I also remember vividly that it never got dark. Not while I was awake, anyway. Shetland has very long days during the summer, being so far north, but with the double summertime that operated during the war, it literally seemed never to get completely dark in all the time I was there.

With so many young men serving in the forces and a desperate need to produce more food and reduce dependence on imports, getting enough people to work on the land became a priority. There was nothing for it but to turn to women. The Women's Land Army (WLA) had existed during the First World War, but had been disbanded after it; it was revived in 1939, with recruitment posters offering a 'healthy, happy job'. At its peak the WLA had 80,000 women, both volunteers and conscripts, working in the fields, milking cows, sawing wood to be used as pit props in mines or forming anti-vermin squads to deal with rats, foxes, rabbits and moles.

Barbara, aged eighteen in 1942, was posted to Crowhurst in Sussex. She was assigned to a threshing gang and sent to various farms, staying for different lengths of time depending on the number of stacks to be threshed out:

In the summer months the gang was split up and we either worked singly or in twos. We also joined large gangs doing gorse clearing and wielded mattocks quite often.

There were hazards for us in the fields during hit-and-run raids over Hastings and also from dropping doodle-bugs which had been hit by anti-aircraft fire or by fighters as they came in over the sea. On one occasion one of our fighter planes blew up overhead and falling debris narrowly missed us.

My billet, a farm cottage, was fairly primitive – not quite like home! No gas or electricity, and one tap over the kitchen sink. A bucket loo was outside. A paraffin lamp stood on the living-room table and we took a candle up to bed with us.

Each day on returning to the billet after work, we took a jug of hot water up to the bedroom to wash the day's grime off. Believe me, there was plenty of that during the threshing season, especially when working on bean or pea stacks. We were allowed to have a bath at the WLA hostel, which was about a mile up the road; this was once a week. It was grand indeed to flop into a bath of hot water with the added luxury of electric light!

Every day we rode to work on our bikes, some days the ride being quite a long one. When the farm or market garden was too far away for us to cycle, we travelled on the old Crowhurst to Sidley and Bexhill rail line or on the main line to Hastings and cycled on from whatever was the nearest station to the job.

One or two of the older farm hands were none too pleased about us working with them and were quite content to watch some of us pulling our insides out whilst attempting to find a way of picking out a stack and also when damp sheaves had begun to grow together (this happened to me when I was a beginner and did not know the ropes. Having almost passed out one day, someone decided to show me the right way to go about it!)

All these years later, I clearly remember with a shudder the time when a rotted bond around a sheaf gave way as I was tugging it whilst standing on the edge of a stack. Somehow or other I managed to keep upright, otherwise it would have meant landing on a moving thresher belt.

There was an element of the Girl Guides about the Land Army: after being employed for at least a year (and having obtained permission from the Land Army County Secretary, who would 'take into account her record of service, including good time keeping'), members could enter for examination in one of a number of proficiency tests:

- Milking and dairy work
- General farm work
- Poultry
- Tractor driving
- Field work
- Outdoor garden and glasshouse work
- Fruit work
- Pest destruction.

Successful completion of practical and oral exams entitled the candidate to wear the Women's Land Army Proficiency

Badge, which would be accompanied by a certificate indicating the branch of work for which the candidate had entered. The Proficiency Badge was to be worn 'on the right-hand lapel of the Land Army overcoat below the Land Army badge, or when the volunteer is without an overcoat, in the centre of the V of the green pullover'.

That overcoat and pullover may have been a Land Girl's uniform, but they weren't her property: not only did they belong to the government, but she was required by the Board of Trade to surrender twenty-four clothing coupons in respect of a year's wear. In the summer of 1944, this represented two-thirds of the year's allowance. The official letter advising the new recruit of her obligations contained this reassurance and this rather paternalistic warning:

As an employed agricultural worker, you will also be entitled to the special supplementary issue of 10 coupons which your employer will be able to draw for you later in the year through your Employment Exchange.

It is important that you should be provident over the spending of the coupons left to you for private use, since if for any reason it should become necessary during the rationing year for you to leave the Land Army you would only get a part refund of the coupons you have surrendered. If you had then used all your other coupons, you might find yourself in difficulties.

Some Land Girls were accommodated on the farms where they worked; others, like Barbara, had to travel considerable distances. On request, they might be allotted a bicycle, but had to wait several weeks to receive it – goodness knows how they were expected to get to work in the meantime. They also had to pay (monthly in advance) a charge of one shilling a week for the privilege.

It wasn't only Land Girls who worked on the farms; later in the war there were prisoners of war, too. John in Yorkshire remembers an occasion when he was about fifteen:

During summer holidays I usually stayed for a week on a farm at Beamsley, near Bolton Abbey, which in turn is near Skipton. There were two POW camps near Skipton, one Italian, one German. Most of the prisoners had been captured in North Africa. The practice was to send groups from each out to help on farms in this very agricultural area. I remember taking tea and a sandwich to a shock-haired Saxon POW, perhaps five years older than me, who was working on the farm. I told him in halting German how the radio said things were going. He said he was lucky to be safe in a sunny English hayfield, but longed to go home to his mother.

This particular POW was much liked by my farming hosts, though there were fraternisation rules which, though I had broken them, explains why the conversation was brief. (That and my German.) Another of the German POWs stayed behind after the war, married a girl in Settle and in time ran his father-in-law's business there, producing the best meat pies in the town.

Valerie in southwest Scotland also has memories of prisoners of war:

There were Italian prisoners-of-war living in a camp about eight miles from where my father had a farm and they came daily to help. My brother reminded me recently that they didn't like working in the rain, which they had to do at times: we had a dairy farm, so there was plenty of hard work. I remember one harvest time I was driving the tractor and trailer (I would have been eleven or twelve years old). The men were loading the trailer with sheaves of corn and my foot slipped off the clutch, with the result that the men fell from the top of the load onto the ground and called me a stupid girl in broken English. Luckily no one was hurt and work went on. I also got a telling off from my father and was told to be more careful.

CHAPTER 7

'YOU'D HAVE THOUGHT WE'D GONE TO AMERICA OR SOMEWHERE'

A lucky few did manage to take holidays, though rarely very far from home and even more rarely in luxurious conditions. If you stayed in a hotel or boarding house, you handed over your ration books so that your hosts could buy enough to feed you – which meant the same unexciting fare and meagre portions you would have had at home.

One way of getting away was to visit a husband or father who was in the forces but stationed somewhere in the UK. Maggie's father was in the RAF and was occasionally able to visit his wife and daughter in Cardiff and subsequently in Barry:

He was posted to Lincolnshire as ground crew. He managed to hitchhike back to see us every now and again – including one memorable Christmas when he broke into next door's chicken coop and stole a chicken so that we could have something more than vegetables for Christmas dinner. I remember Mrs Diamond next door being very suspicious because one of her hens had apparently run away but had remembered to bolt the door of the hen house behind it.

Then one summer Father suggested that we go up to stay with him. We rented a cottage and he took us out to the aerodrome to see the bomber he was working on. I remember quite clearly that you got into it through the bottom of the nose. There was a ladder down from the entrance; Father went up and said, 'Come on', so I climbed up too and went inside and just stood there. I was frightened that it was going to take off and take me with it, so I quickly scrambled down the ladder again.

We were staying in a pretty village with a stream running through it and the highlight of that holiday was that there was a sweetshop by the stream. They made wonderful liquorice toffee. A penny a bag – I loved it and I seemed to spend the whole summer eating liquorice toffee.

Pauline, another whose dad was in the RAF, also used to visit him during the summer holidays:

My mother was in the hat trade – she used to have boxes of hats brought home to trim them and I would put them on my knee and pretend I could do it as well: I was quite intrigued with stitching hat bands and so on.

Then someone would come with a horse and cart and take them away. I think we went away for the only two weeks' holiday Mum got each year.

Dad was stationed in many different parts of Britain, so sometimes we would go and stay wherever he was billeted. My favourite place was Mundesley in Norfolk. We stayed in a wooden bungalow – it was quite spacious but there was no electricity, so we had to light paraffin lamps. Mr and Mrs Willer, who owned it, grew all their own vegetables and had chickens, ducks, turkeys, pigs and rabbits, a dog called Bruce and a cat called Felix. I spent most of my time with the rabbits and didn't realise some of them were gradually disappearing! There was a little black and white one that I loved, then all of a sudden he was gone. I asked Mr Willer where it was and was appalled when he said, 'We've eaten it.'

Mrs Willer had very long hair, which she plaited and wound up the plaits on each side of her cheeks. As a small child I thought they were ear phones. The geese and turkeys used to wander about loose and in the mornings they'd wake you up. One day I asked Mr Willer what he fed the turkeys on and he replied, 'Brick dust and onions, me dear.' I have never forgotten that – for ages I thought it was true!

Another time Dad was stationed at High Flats in Yorkshire and billeted at Birdsedge, near Huddersfield, on the edge of the moors. The place we stayed in had big iron gates and looked a bit like an estate, but I think it must have been a farm. I can remember the dry stone walls. There were quite a lot of people living there and the lady used to make Yorkshire pudding in a big enamel basin like the kind you'd wash your hands in in the sink. She made pies like that, too, in enormous dishes, because she was catering for so many people. The toilets were in a big shed down the slope of the hill and when you got there it was a bench with four holes in. You did what you had to do and it dropped down and there were big doors at the back – I suppose they had to clear it out somehow.

The lady at the farm had a daughter who was married and lived down the road; she had a boy and a girl who were about the same age as my brother and me and we used to go up on the moors and pick cowslips. So that was quite a nice place, but I think we only went there once. We got there by train, which meant changing at Crewe – I can remember sitting on Crewe platform and it being ages and ages before the next train.

Charlotte's family also followed her father to an RAF posting:

We had a seaside holiday once during the war. My mother and brother and I went by train from Derbyshire to Wells-next-the-Sea in Norfolk, near where Father was stationed. I remember there were defences – I don't suppose we could go on any of the beaches, but I don't remember in detail. I do remember we arrived, got out of the train and then realised that our luggage was still on it. I can still see the back of the train going away into the distance and remember the horror of knowing our luggage was still on it. Heaven knows how that was sorted out. But it's rather extraordinary to think of a holiday in the middle of the war anyway, isn't it?

… as did Brenda's:

When I was about seven or eight Dad was stationed at Cannock in Staffordshire. He had a friend who lived nearby and we went up there and stayed with them so that we could see Dad. I remember I had to call the lady 'Auntie Maud'. Dad wasn't there all the time, but he could get away sometimes to be with us.

Another time we thought he was going to be posted overseas, so we went down to somewhere near Taunton to say goodbye. But then they found that he had something wrong with his leg and he wasn't considered fit enough to go. So he stayed in England for the rest of the war, up near Bury St Edmunds, working 'on the ground' on Hurricanes and Lancasters. We never visited there, and the time in Taunton was only for a weekend or so, so going to Cannock was the only real 'holiday'.

Bridget's family went on holiday from a London suburb to the Chilterns – all of thirty-five miles, but a different world:

In 1943 we rented a rather ghastly little cottage down near Ivinghoe Beacon. It had no running water, so you had to get water from a well, and there was an outside loo. I can't think it would have been much of a holiday for my mother – she'd have been better off in our own house, really, with three small children.

The following year we had a proper holiday, at Abersoch on the Llyn Peninsula in Wales. Somebody lent my father a bungalow on the coast there and we actually saw the sea and bathed off beaches. There was no land mines or barbed wire – I don't think anyone thought the Germans would get right round there to try to land. But I remember that it took about twelve hours and we had to change trains three times – running from one platform to another with all your luggage and a baby: no wonder people didn't go away. I can remember sitting on somebody's lap most of the way because there weren't any seats.

Trains were always jam-packed. It was a nightmare if you wanted to go and spend a penny, because you had to push past people standing with their suitcases in the corridor, and I don't think there was any food or drinks available. So whether you had to dash off to the buffet at Crewe Station to get a cup of something, I don't know, but there weren't plastic cups with lids, so you had to drink it where they gave it to you, and you wouldn't think there'd be time. My mother always took food with us. I remember a comedian called Ethel Revenell who did a skit where she was running a station buffet; someone had dared ask her what was in the bun. 'If it doesn't have legs, it's a currant,' was the reply. And that was about it, really, for a station buffet.

For those who couldn't go away, there was an attempt to bring holidays to you. A government scheme called Holidays at Home encouraged local authorities to provide a range of amusements, from a fine local history pageant in Bermondsey, South London, to three weeks of sports, games, donkey rides, concert parties, military bands, model railway and yacht contests in Huddersfield. One (inland) authority is even said to have brought in enough sand to turn its parks into temporary beaches.

June remembers some of the events that were put on in Andover:

Before the war there used to be an annual summer carnival. We didn't have that during the war, but there were various events put on under the 'Holidays at Home' scheme. I think it was the committee that usually organised the carnival that arranged things: there was a talent competition, fetes, bazaars and lots of dancing. We used to do a lot of country dancing, and when the Americans were over, gathering in strength for D-Day, they used to have bands with them, which would come and play for our dancing, outdoors. They were all in uniform, but they were professional musicians and they could play all sorts of things, so we gave them the music and they played the familiar tunes that we were used to for the country dancing.

On August Bank Holiday the Walled Meadow was the scene of a Flower, Fruit and Vegetable Show and a Fur and Feather Show, housed in two large marquees.

The Flower, Fruit and Veg had a special section for children's handicrafts and art, so my friend Joy and I entered various items which we had made in art classes. We both won several prizes.

There were special pictures at the cinema, too. We had three cinemas in Andover and they changed the programmes twice a week, so you could go six times a week and see six different films if you were that keen. I wasn't as dedicated as that, but I remember seeing a lot of comedies by people like George Formby – he was always popular – and the Crazy Gang.

Evelyn in Kendal was less impressed by Holidays at Home. Writing to her husband in August 1942, she said:

August Bank Holiday Monday, and nothing worthwhile about it, but the receipt of your air-graph 15/7/42. Took 'cherubs' to pictures on Saturday afternoon to see Walt Disney's 'Dumbo'. Terrible thunderstorm on Sunday, and heavy rain all day. Holiday week in this town – a farce, I think! Nearly all cricket and golf matches.

Three days later:

Holiday-at-home week in Kendal. Took 'cherubs' to Carnival Dance in Abbott Hall yesterday evening, after having watched bowls competition. Cherubs think they should go here, there and everywhere. Made me very sick and 'fed-up' to see so many men just sat, or playing bowls. Made me even more sick to count *twenty* men officiating at one end of race tracks of children's sports. Martin sat at the table all afternoon. And this is what you are fighting for.

In August 1942, Rose wrote to her sister that the Women's Home Defence (a sort of female Home Guard), of which she was a member, had secured a rifle range. This not only enabled women to practise shooting but became a centre for social activities, notably a dance. Having decided on a venue…

…now the thing is to find an orchestra, which is rather difficult these days. In addition to which is the question of refreshments, and the woman who seems to be taking matters into her own hands as she has had some experience in these small dances, suggests that members are charged 1/- for their tickets and to bring 3 cakes each. Other people will be charged 1/6. I shall have to get down to work these figures out presently. Then of course is the question of tea and coffee and especially milk. I suppose we shall have to have tinned milk, but I don't care for it much. Our ration comes down again on Sunday to less than ½ a pint a day each. That means we shall have to start portioning it out again at home. Since May we have been having as much as we like.

Despite these concerns, the dance was a great success:

We had 12 raffle prizes, all sorts of things provided by a member, baskets of fruit, new laid eggs, a big cake, etc. … For the spot prizes for the ladies I bought a ½ lb box of chocs (which took my month's ration of coupons), for the men cigarettes and iodine pencils. It got to seven o'c before we could turn round, and all the cakes and refreshments were scattered all over the cloakroom, which was men's and women's combined, and an unholy mess. Then someone said someone was asking for me, and it was Sir Edward Campbell, our M.P. who I had written to and who came along for half an hour although he was due at another function. Very sporting of him. The band turned up but had to go home again for their music, but anyway, no one very much turned up until 7.30 so it didn't matter. Sir Edward and I had the first dance.…Then things got warmed up and we got more packed every minute. At 8.30 I had the first spot prize. At 9 I made a little speech, telling the women about what we did (which brought in 5 new members the following Tuesday) and then we had the interval. The refreshment interval I am afraid was a bit of a mess. Next time I will have it my way…

After the interval I was busy in the cloakroom, mostly wondering what to do with about 200 sandwiches, dishes of cakes and lord knows what, so first I put on a tray half a dozen big cakes that hadn't been cut and took them in and auctioned them.

Wendy in Surrey recalls various summer entertainments:

Fetes were a big feature of summer. They took place at school and in the local rec. They were a big deal. We kept rabbits and I used to enter one for the pet show. One year when I was about eight my school entered a pageant, another big deal. We enacted 'The Pied Piper of Hamlyn' and walked through the streets for what seemed like miles. I was the poor lame boy and had to hop on crutches through the town, dressed in a hot, tight-fitting jacket and breeches made of blue felt. At the back of the procession I was miserable.

Public swimming baths were closed, but our local tennis club had a pool that opened for swimming lessons. I remember summer weather as being warm and sunny. But swimming in a freezing pool and drying with sopping wet towels was no fun. Because water was saved for the fire services the pool water was never changed, and its green murkiness was a favourite home for frogs. Thank goodness we didn't have to swim with our faces in the water – we did a head-up breaststroke. We were taught by the grim and demanding tennis coach, a red-headed, permanently tanned tyrant. The learning aid consisted of inflatable canvas 'water wings' attached by a strap that went under the chest. As we progressed a rope was tied to us, we started at the deep end with our torturer at the shallow end holding the rope to prevent us going under or, if we were too slow, dragging us through the water.

My parents were busy and we children enjoyed a fair amount of freedom in the summer holidays: in the garden, walking on the Downs or cycling (there were no cars on the roads). We didn't go out much as a family or take family holidays. I do remember one time my mother took all four of us to Kew Gardens on the bus. It cost a penny to go through the turnstile. We were allowed to climb to the top of the Pagoda – amazing! It had come all the way from China. The monkey puzzle trees were amazing too.

Connie was able to go on one holiday from Liverpool:

We didn't go on holidays as such – no one went to Spain the way they did later – and of course you never knew from one day to the next if the railway line was going to have been bombed or anything like that, so we didn't even go to North Wales, which was so close at hand, until the very end of the war. I had a cousin, much older than me, who was a schoolteacher. She was sent to Mold, in North Wales, and as a treat we went on the train to visit her. She took us all around Mold and that was a great thrill to us – you'd have thought we'd gone to America or somewhere, we were so excited. It was wonderful.

Mostly, though, our 'holidays' were visiting friends, and possibly staying overnight. Going to the cinema on a Saturday was our big night out. I remember Betty Grable, Frank Sinatra. And I remember the queues. You always had to queue to get in.

She remembers enjoying the theatre, too, but her first love was ballet:

> Mum made all my ballet clothes for me: most of my clothing coupons went towards material for my costumes. I must have worn my sister's hand-me-downs the rest of the time. For classes I had a sleeveless satin dress with a round neck and matching waistband and knickers. Every year we put on a dance with a different theme and one year the theme was the sky at night. I was dressed in a black tutu with a gold moon sewn into the front of it.
>
> We sometimes performed at the Crane Hall in Hanover Street – it's the Epstein Theatre now, but in those days the front was a shop selling pianos. Buried in the back were studios and a proper little theatre. I particularly remember the curtains. They were swept to the sides and up, as though they had a tie-back, like on window curtains today. I was very impressed. For one performance my uncle built a large picture frame and covered it in crinoline material. I was the 'Crinoline Girl' (as always, my mother made the costume). There were other girls in other frames and we all 'came alive' and danced. My mother saved a piece of that crinoline material and covered a coat hanger in it, which I still have.
>
> At home, my sister Blanche played the piano, so people would come and we'd all sing around the piano. We had the gramophone and we played records of Frank Sinatra and people like that. I used to go dinner dances with

Blanche, who was three years older than me, but my mother didn't like us going too far from home because of the sirens. If you heard the siren, you had to head for a shelter. We went to dancing contests, too, and I remember winning certificates, but not medals. There was no metal to spare for giving out that sort of medal.

Sue and her sisters were also able to go to dancing classes:

We used to get the train into Tunbridge Wells for dancing classes, which I realise now was very posh. Of course, as children you aren't aware of posh or not posh, that sort of thing floats over you. But the woman who taught us was called Betty Vacani and she had taught the royal children – the future queen and Princess Margaret – and, later, she taught Prince Charles and Princess Anne.

For most people, though, the cinema was the main source of entertainment. Sylvia in Luton was a devotee:

The films used to run consecutively, so you didn't go in at a specific time as you do now; you would often go in in the middle, so you'd remember where you'd started, and when that bit came around again you'd go out. If you wanted to, you could just sit there and watch it over again, but most people didn't – maybe they felt honour bound to leave, because of the queues.

At this time, although I was sixteen and had started nursing, I looked very young. There was a film called

The Lamp Still Burns, based on Monica Dickens' novel *One Pair of Feet* – it was about nursing during the war and I was eager to see it. They wouldn't let me in, because for some reason it was an A certificate, which meant that a child had to be accompanied by an adult, and the people at the cinema didn't believe I was old enough to see it on my own. I remember being very put out. I did have an ID card, of course, but unfortunately it was a child's one. This must have been shortly after I turned sixteen, because you got an adult ID when you were sixteen and mine can't have arrived. I remember arguing with the people at the box office, but it didn't make any difference.

Jeanne and her mother went to 'the pictures' too:

My mother and I were great for going to the cinema during the war – at least twice a week, and I used to get *Picturegoer* magazine, so I could read all about the films. There were James Mason and Stewart Granger: James Mason was a bit of a baddy and Stewart Granger was a bit of a wet. Then there was Margaret Lockwood, with lots of heaving bosom. And I saw *Gone with the Wind*, with Vivien Leigh saying, 'I'll never go hungry again' and making a dress out of the curtains: it all rang quite true at the time. We thought *Gone with the Wind* was wonderful, though I remember seeing it again recently and thinking how long it was.

Morecambe also had a theatre that we sometimes

went to. I remember a musical, probably Ivor Novello's *The Dancing Years*, which is set in Vienna. One of the actors came on in Tyrolean-style shorts, lederhosen. He was rather camp and there were lots of servicemen up in the balcony and they all screamed with laughter. The actor just said, 'Close the balcony. We won't have any more of those people', because they were making fun of him. I was very impressed by this at the time.

With theatres and concert halls closed and precious artworks having been sent to Wales for safekeeping, culture-loving Londoners had particular reason to be grateful to the pianist Myra Hess. Starting only a few weeks after war broke out and running from Monday to Friday for the duration, she organised almost 2,000 low-cost lunchtime concerts in the otherwise empty National Gallery. Her purpose was 'to give spiritual solace to those who are giving all to combat the evil'.

Concert halls and theatres were, of course, as susceptible to bombing as anywhere else, and the Queen's Hall in Langham Place was hit on the night of 10 May 1941, the worst night of bombing in London, and burned to the ground. Paul, whose mother's canteen was on duty outside the remains of the hall the following day, recalls a story he was told later by the pianist Moura Lympany. She had been due to play a concert there on the 11th:

They moved the whole event to the Royal Academy of Music, at the Duke's Hall in Marylebone Road. Of course, most of the instruments were portable, so they wouldn't have been left in the hall, but they were a bit short of double basses. They managed to rescue some of them, but not all. And they did the programme exactly as it would have been, and had a full house.

The Queen's Hall had been home to the Proms and one of the few things to survive the blast was a bronze bust of Proms founder Henry Wood. 'So I'm still here,' he remarked, and had the statue taken to the Albert Hall, where that year's Proms season duly opened on 12 July. The first item to be performed on that first night was Elgar's Cockayne Overture 'In London Town', described as 'a love letter to the capital'; the programme notes refer to 'London's imperturbable cheerfulness'.

For the troops, entertainment was provided by the Entertainments National Service Association or ENSA, set up at the start of the war. Performers who took part in ENSA entertainments ranged from the 'Forces' Sweetheart', singer Vera Lynn, to popular comedians such as Tommy Trinder and serious actors such as Sybil Thorndike. The impressive roster of names also included Flanagan and Allen, George Formby, Margaret Rutherford and Noël Coward. Not every ENSA production was of a high standard, though: its initials were often said to stand for 'Every Night Something Awful'.

Kate joined ENSA after training at RADA. Her company toured the north of England, performing a drama by Aimée and Philip Stuart called *Nine Till Six* to audiences of British and American service folk. July 1944 found her in

Scarborough for a fortnight and sending dirty laundry home
to her mother in London:

> Ever so sorry to burden you with this washing but I
> just cannot do it here. We have only a washstand in our
> room and the landlady is busy in the kitchen cooking
> for about 24 people. I just scrounged enough water to
> wash my vest.
>
> These digs are *so* clean and are really very good. Nancy
> and I have the best bedroom, too. And it's very central,
> near the sea and the town.
>
> There are millions of people here. Yesterday and
> Sunday the beach looked quite pre-war – even a Punch
> & Judy & deck chairs & spades & pails. The people in
> the north are lucky, I expect many of them get a holiday
> like this every year.
>
> There's rock & picture post cards & a cliff lift.
>
> We have to walk quite a way before we come to any
> deserted beach but we found a nice spot in the end and
> sunned ourselves.
>
> We had a glorious drive last night through dales and
> woody hills – it's very lovely country here.

The next stop, Darlington, was less appealing. Not only
that, but *Nine Till Six* wasn't the light-hearted variety show
audiences were used to:

> The hotel is awful – dirty and dingy and it positively
> stinks – of dogs mainly, and stale food. We have pigs

beneath our window, but they don't smell, they only snort. The food is very good, though, despite the smell from the kitchen quarter. So…

Last night's outing was terrible. It was so unbelievably awful that we thought we were having an actor's nightmare – like not knowing your lines and having half a mile to run and being late for your cue. Well, it was a village hall we found ourselves in. We've been playing many of these lately. There were no tabs [front curtains], the lighting was no better than 6 candle power really it wasn't. The doors in the hall had to be opened to let light onto the stage! The stage was surrounded by camouflage netting – filthy dirty and smelly – which we had to remove. Anyway – we could have borne with all this but – they'd never had a play before. The Entertainments Officer didn't even know it *was* a play, & the whole audience sat the whole way through without a sound & without any applause until Eric told them the play had finished. Even the cat must have found it tiresome – she had 4 beautiful black kittens during the show.

In the absence of theatre or concerts, there were dance halls. Eileen was working in a factory but still living with her parents. She remembers going out dancing when she was about fifteen:

That used to be a sneaky thing for me because I wasn't allowed to go to dance halls. There was a very popular dance hall called the Hammersmith Palais and I used to sneak there sometimes on a lie. I can understand now why my parents wanted to know where I was. If I went out anywhere it was, 'Where are you going?' Being a teenager I resented this, but I understand it now.

We'd also go to milk bars, as they were called then, just to meet friends and talk to people. We were too young for pubs, and in a milk bar you could have a lemonade or something like that and make it last all night. You more or less had to, because money was very scarce. This would just have been at the weekend, because we worked till six every evening, so by the time you'd been home and had your food it was too late to go out – we started work again at half-past seven in the morning. So going out was really only on a Saturday night.

For those who stayed at home in the evening, the radio or 'wireless' was the main form of entertainment and of news. Connie remembers how important this was:

We didn't have any telephones, we didn't have any TV; we had the wireless and that was our lifesaver. We got very little news really, and we never got a weather forecast. Today, with all the new technologies, foreigners know exactly what's going on here, but in those days they didn't have that.

Bridget in Wembley Park remembers the radio as a source of other information, too:

We used to sit in the evening and listen to the wireless and it would go off when the planes came over the coast. Simply shut down. So we knew something was going to happen. We would be in our pyjamas and we had to go out to the shelter in the garden, carrying a little suitcase with our school uniform for the next morning, in case the house was bombed and we didn't have anything to put on. This seemed always to happen when there was something on the radio that my sister wanted to hear – *Monday Night at Eight*, which was a variety programme with music and comedy and all sorts of things, or something like that.

Jeanne recalls one particularly rousing occasion when listening to the wireless:

When we were staying in the caravan we went up to the farm every night to listen to the news at nine o'clock, because they had a radio and we didn't. I've noted in my diary on 8 September 1943: 'Listened to Churchill's speech. Stupendous news at 9 pm. Forward to victory!' That was the night we learned that Italy had surrendered.

Billy in Bathgate, West Lothian, a resourceful ten-year-old, made a great deal of his own entertainment:

With no going on holidays, we children had to make our own enjoyment-cum-recreation. Rabbiting with my grandpa, fishing for minnows in Reily's burn, swimming in the pool at the side of the mill, digging play trenches on the Mair and playing soldiers were all part of my summer activities. Then there was rummaging about Wolfe's coup – basically a rubbish tip – near the English kirk. This was the source of one of our more enterprising adventures.

With petrol scarce and fewer cars on the road, car batteries became defunct and were thrown into the coup. I had a bundle of *World of Wonder* magazines that interested me more than a school reading book, so maybe the following enterprise emanated from that source. We boys seemed to know that car batteries contained dangerous acid and lead (not yet recognised as a danger to health). So we smashed the batteries, avoided the liquid and extracted the lead filaments. The coup was all humfs and hows [humps and hollows], as we called them, so we could get up to all sorts of ploys and be fairly undetected. On one occasion we gathered fragments of coal and other combustibles and lit a fire. An old tin can acted as a crucible and we melted the lead panels quite easily. I can remember looking at the grey scum floating on the top and thought of trying to gather it on a stick – or hold it back as we poured the molten metal. When we did pour, delight of delights, the brilliantly silver liquid slipped out from under the scum, leaving it behind. We poured it into boot-polish lids and ended up with ingots of pure lead. I had an idea of how metal casting was done from my magazines, so here was a case in which to cast our own lead soldiers.

Remember, we had few toys by this time, 1943–44. As a boy of ten my capacity for teaching myself was coming to the fore.

Toy soldiers – method:

1. Fill a matchbox with clay and smear the top flat.
2. Persuade Curly Nagle to bring out his rosary and press the crucifix into the clay.
3. Melt lead.
4. Pour molten lead into the crucifix impression. Of course the metal could not be controlled to pour just to the edge of the mould, thus the cast, though perfect, was blobby round the edges. Back to the drawing board – I needed a riser.
5. Remove base from a second matchbox and introduce clay into the remainder, smear top and bottom as flat as possible.
6. Place riser box on top of mould box and, using a bit of slate pencil, aim a hole down into centre of cross impression. Tidy up edges and pour the lead down the spout.

The result was a resounding success with a cross of comparatively clean edges and a little riser, which I did not cut off. The crucifix castings are now the property of Bennie Museum in Bathgate. Only one improved version was cast and I don't remember repeating the ploy ever again.

Tony, five years old when war broke out, remembers simpler games:

Down towards town from where I lived there was a big park, with terraced houses on three sides – it had swings and roundabouts and that sort of thing, and because there was a school opposite they built some shelters underground. There weren't many air raids during the day, though there were a lot at night, but we were always aware that they might come any time. So when we weren't playing in the street just outside our houses, we were allowed to go down to the 'rec', because our parents knew there was somewhere for us to shelter if we needed to. The threat of raids certainly curtailed what we were allowed to do. I loved swimming, but the public swimming pool was too far away and I wasn't allowed to go. But we played football or cricket; we'd take a bottle of water or orange juice and some jam sandwiches and stay out all day. As long as we were home for tea, our mums seemed to be quite happy.

Then in the evenings, because it was still light, we were allowed to play outside on the pavement. One of the games was Hopscotch. You drew eight squares in a pattern in chalk, then threw a stone into one of the squares and hopped about trying to pick it up. Given that we lived on a chalk hill, that was one thing we were never short of. After we'd finished we had to come inside, fetch a bucket of water, wash it off and start all over again the following evening.

We also used to play with a 'whip and top'. You could buy them in a shop, or you could make them. There was a chap round the corner who was a carpenter and because he had lathes he used to make a lot of these tops, all different designs. The whip was just a stick with a long piece of string on it. Down the other end of the string you left about an inch and tied a knot, then frayed it all out. The top was a circular piece of wood, like a cotton-reel, that came to a point. This man used to paint them in different colours. Sometimes they looked like a mushroom; sometimes they were just straight, with ridges round them – different designs that he did on his lathe, but they always had to come to a point at the top. At the bottom he'd hammer in something like a boot stud, just a blob of metal with a point on it. You wrapped the string around it, got hold of the stick and flicked it so that the string came undone. As it did that, it twisted the top round and you'd follow it up and down the street and flick it again with the whip so that it kept twisting and you kept chasing it. If you were very clever you could pick the top up in your fingers and twist it and drop it down and it would start spinning – just like the sort of tops that you can buy now for kids, only they have the built-in mechanism and we had to make our own.

Scooters were very popular: very different to the scooters you see today. They were basically metal with a wooden platform; they didn't have a brake on them. You just kept pedalling with one foot. I had a scooter like that. We also had a desk that we kept tucked away in a cupboard in the kitchen: we kept crayons and paper and things like that in it. This desk had a fold-up chair with crossed legs that had a bar across each one. The legs folded up, but when they were opened out the chair fitted neatly across the wooden platform on the scooter. If you were good at balancing, you could sit on it: it turned into something more like a bike that you pedalled with one foot. It was mine, but I didn't get many goes on it, because everyone else wanted to try. We lived on a bit of a hill, so you could just scoot round the corner and then push the scooter back up again and scoot back down.

Pauline's activities also included cricket:

There was a lovely field behind one friend's house, but it was attached to the cemetery – I think it was being kept for when the cemetery needed more space, though it's got houses on it now. We weren't really supposed to go in there. But we used to go in and play cricket. Occasionally the cemetery man would come and chase us out – he was a big, tall man, with a black coat and a homburg hat, and we were a bit scared of him. We used to post someone as a lookout and if they called out, 'Here comes the cemetery man,' we all had to scatter. Then as soon as the man had gone, we'd go back again.

Double summer time played tricks with the schedules. Pauline recalls:

I can remember being out in the street playing and my mother saying, 'You must come in now.' I said, 'But it's still light' and she said, 'It's nearly eleven o'clock.' That can't have been a school night, because goodness knows how I would have got up in the morning if it had been, but it seemed very unfair to me.

John in Weymouth also remembers childhood games, some of them dictated by the unique geography of the area, which gave it strategic importance:

There are the remains of three castles along the coastline here, one at Nothe, one at Sandsfoot and one at Portland – built by Henry VIII to keep out the French. That was all a bit of a joke, apparently, because the distance between Portland Castle and Sandsfoot Castle was so great and the range of the cannons so limited that the French fleet could have parked in the middle of Portland Bay, out of range of the cannons, and come ashore at night and raise mayhem. Fortunately, they never did.

But there's a nice sandy cove just north of Sandsfoot Castle and lots of other sandy beaches round Weymouth Bay – very fine sand, wonderful places for the enemy to land. Most of the rest of the coastline nearby is cliffs, so nobody was going to land there, and at Chesil Beach the sea comes in with huge waves and such an undertow that nothing could land there either. So these few flat beaches, giving access to the hinterland, were immensely important.

Before the war we had enjoyed all of our leisure time pretty much playing around on the cliff-tops – there was a cliff walk near Sandsfoot Castle, very close to where I lived – or running around the rocks, building sandcastles, paddling and so forth; if the tide was out, there was a nice stretch of sandy beach where we could play cricket. That's the sort of thing we did before the war, on a day-to-day basis, both in the holidays and after school or at weekends. Portland Harbour was one of the homes to the Home Fleet; from time to time before the war liners used to put in there overnight and cause great waves when they left, swamping the beaches where we might have been playing.

The other influential thing about this part of the world was the presence of the Whitehead Torpedo Works. This was the principal source of torpedoes for the British fleet and was therefore of interest to the Germans. The torpedoes were tested in the harbour, launched from a point on the harbour wall. They were supposed to go under a series of rafts, and then the people doing the testing would measure how long they took and that sort of thing.

The changes that happened during the war were first of all that the beaches were separated from the mainland by barbed wire. And all along the Weymouth Bay beaches, those very good landing places, there were anti-tank barricades made out of scaffolding. They were about thirty to sixty feet offshore and that interfered with swimming and so forth. We could still get to the beach within Portland Harbour, because the defence there was the harbour wall itself; access to the harbour was quite heavily protected.

My father worked at the torpedo factory, in the office. When war started I was six and my sisters were ten, eight and three. We three older ones used to play a bit together on the beach, but by the time war started I was more likely to be with other boys my age, throwing stones in the water or playing with things we called 'puggy sticks': there were clay deposits in the cliffs and we would make balls of clay, which we could flick great distances. All sorts of childish games like that.

Initially, not a lot happened to interfere with us playing in that way, so when there was a holiday, when school was out, that's what we did. But after a while some of the areas where we used to play became training grounds for the military. There used to be a nice patch of grass by Sandford Castle, where we could kick a ball about or knock off an old tennis ball with an old cricket bat, but it was taken over by the trainee commandos. They used it to practise how to get over barbed-wire fences. First of all, they put up huge fences, three or four coils of barbed wire to start with, then three coils on top of that and two more on top of that, so we had to play elsewhere.

One of the commandos, for reasons I couldn't understand, brought his tennis racquet with him. That struck us as a bit posh – not many ordinary people played tennis in those days. But when he left, he left the racquet behind, so that was a plaything during the war – there was no traffic, so we could just go out into the road and play catch, hitting the ball to each other, with no net, of course, and only one racquet. We must have taken it in turns to use it, because we only ever had the one.

Audrey in Weymouth recalls the occasional party at school:

Looking back, I think they were very basic – a few party games and that was about it. But there was one time that the local fishmonger tried to make ice cream for us. I don't know that it was very successful, but it was better than anyone else would have managed – he was the only person in the whole of Weymouth who had a fridge.

I remember it always being very sunny – maybe that's just a typical childhood memory, of sunny days. I used to go over to Chafey's Lake to collect tadpoles; I'd bring them home and watch them grow little legs. I don't remember them ever turning into frogs, but I know that my father took a great interest, so perhaps he took them back to the lake and released them.

Anne from Newport has fond memories of summer holidays spent close to home:

I remember the summers as absolutely great: we had picnics and we used to go foraging for blackberries down at the lighthouse, which was a real treat. We took one of Dad's walking sticks so that we could reach the high branches. The blackberries were so big and so lovely, and we got mushrooms that were big enough to fill a frying pan – they were really gorgeous. We had relatives who had a farm, so when we'd been up to visit them we'd bring back some home-cured bacon, and just a few pieces of that in the pan with the mushrooms were wonderful.

My mother and I used to work in the garden at home and I would pick the beans and the peas and the raspberries, because as a small child that was the sort of job I could do. We would get as brown as berries just being in our own garden. But I also had a great-aunt who lived near Bridgend and we had lovely summer holidays there. We were able to play on the beach. It was always sunny – they were real summer holidays.

Maggie in Barry was close enough to the beach to be able to go whenever the weather was fine:

On sunny days we used to pack up the pram. It was one of those great big, old-fashioned ones with a semi-circular base: you could lift the mattress out and fill the bottom with goodness knows what, put the top back on, put the baby in and away you go. And we'd walk down to the beach at Barry Island.

There was a horse and cart on the beach and you could pay sixpence or something like that and go for a ride in the cart, backwards and forwards across the beach. I was digging holes in the sand with my little sister Elizabeth, who was about eighteen months old, and we dug one so big that she could fit inside it. The horse and cart were standing in their usual place, waiting for the next customer, and suddenly the horse was stung by a bee and it bolted – along the sand towards us. Mother saw it and managed to grab Elizabeth away; moments later, the horse came dashing up and both it and the cart went right into the hole where she had been sitting. They managed to catch it after that, but if Mother had been any slower, Elizabeth would have been killed.

There was another beach on the other side of Porthkerry Woods – Cold Knap, it was called. It was pebbly and completely different from the sandy beach at Barry. Among other things the water was freezing – I guess the water was warmer where it had passed over the sand, but I often wonder if it was called Cold Knap because the water was so blooming cold.

Having a baby sister was a mixed blessing as far as Maggie was concerned. Elizabeth was six years younger and 'a terrible baby':

She wouldn't let Mother out of her sight and on the rare occasions when Father came back, she used to cry and cry and cry. Sometimes he'd be there just for one night and he'd be saying, 'I'll be glad to get back to camp and get some sleep.'

I had a friend up the road called Joan Jones, and she had a baby brother who was about the same age as Elizabeth. One time when I was going up to see Joan,

Mother insisted I take the baby with me in her pram. I complained, of course – the times that pram fell over is nobody's business. I really hated pushing it. It was a lovely sunny day, but I remembering pushing Elizabeth up the hill and thinking, 'I'm fed up with this.' I had wanted a little brother, and I knew that Joan had wanted a sister, so as I walked along, I decided what I should do. I can see it quite clearly – they had a green back door, I knocked on it and Mrs Jones answered.

'I've been thinking,' I said. 'Joan wanted a sister and I wanted a brother, and she's got a brother and I've got a sister. So perhaps we could swap?'

'Have you spoken to your mother about this?' asked Mrs Jones, quite seriously.

'Oh, she won't mind,' I said firmly.

But she suggested that we should think a bit more about it, and then she noticed my knees.

'Where have you been?' she said. 'Your knees are filthy.' I must have been playing in the garden, I suppose, because my knees were covered in dirt, but I said, 'It's sunburn.' I don't think Mrs Jones was impressed with me that day. I certainly never heard any more about swapping Elizabeth for Joan's brother.

Anne in Newport remembers that it wasn't *always* sunny on Barry Island:

The first summer holiday I remember when Dad was home, perhaps 1944 or '45, all along the coastline they had put great rolls of barbed wire, six-foot high and rolled up like sausage rolls. They were huge things and they went the length of the Barry Island coastline, along that beautiful bay. They'd cut a small opening in one of them so that you could walk down to the beach through it. Of course it seemed very high to me because I was small: it was way above my head and we walked through this wire corridor, then down the steps on to the beach. We only had about three days while Dad was on leave and it was hammering with rain, but I was determined I was going to dig in the sand. So there I was in my mac, with a bucket and a spade, making a castle. It was marvellous.

We used to go to Barry Island on Sunday School trips, from the church; we used to commandeer an entire steam train and steam right on to the island. (It isn't an island, in fact, it's a peninsula, so you could get there easily enough by train.) If you were trying to go the other way when a train came in, it was like a tide of people coming towards you, because *everybody* went to Barry Island – everybody from Newport, everybody from Cardiff and from the valleys too. The beach was *full*. Even during the war.

There was a sort of stall at the top of the beach selling 'trays for the beach'. We always took a flask, with a cork in the top of it and a bit of greaseproof paper to help seal it. And frankly the tea tasted horrible because it was stewed, but it was much cheaper than buying refreshments when you got there. But some of the posher people took one of these 'trays', which included a great big brown earthenware, usually chipped, teapot and earthenware mugs. You paid a deposit and took the tray and the teapot down onto the beach with you. I thought this was wonderful – it was always my ambition to have one of those, but I never did.

When I went with the Sunday School, the deacons and the elders of the church all got themselves seated in a big circle near the back wall, which was painted with numbers. We were allowed to go backwards and forwards, but we had to memorise our number so that we knew where to come back to and find the right people. Those numbers are still on the wall at Barry Island now.

My aunt had knitted me a ginger woollen bathing costume. Because wool was in short supply and was always being recycled, she must have unravelled a jumper or something, then washed the wool and rolled it up in balls, and of course the wool was crinkly. I put it on and played in the sand and that was fine, but then I went down to the sea and you can imagine what happened. It fell down to my ankles. I went back to my mother clutching up these yards and yards of soggy ginger wool – I felt quite humiliated.

Travelling on the train was exciting, though my mother always said, 'Don't look out of the window, you'll get a smut in your eye.' If I did, she'd screw up the corner of her hanky and lick it and hoick the smut out – it was quite barbaric. You opened and shut the windows with great leather straps perforated like belts, which you hooked over a little brass knob on the door itself to keep the window at the level you wanted it. The seats were a sort of uncut moquette and underneath they must have been straw, because if you bounced up and down as a child you could produce *clouds* of dust. The first thing that happened when we got off the train was that Mother would want to put me in the bath.

Bridget wrote to her sister about a family outing from Wembley Park on the August Bank Holiday of 1944:

As yesterday was Bank Holiday and Daddy was at home, Mummy thought that we could take our lunch and go for a picnic in a wood at Chalfont and then walk on to Latimer.

We started off from home at 11.30. At Wembley Park there were lots of people but we all got a seat in the train. At Harrow there were millions of people on the station already. The train when it came in was packed. Mummy had a seat and so did I; one woman had the most enormous collie dog which took almost the whole floor and barked all the time. There were about twenty people in the carriage, but at Rickmansworth most of them got out. When we got to Chalfont we walked through a wheat field and then got to the wood. We had lunch in a lovely hollow, which was covered with leaves. We stayed there for about half an hour and then walked about a mile and reached Latimer. It's a fairly old place, but very nice. Daddy thought it would be nice to go and pay a call on Aunt Emm. It was simply baking hot. To get there, we walked along a road, then up a hill through a wood, along a road through a footpath, across the bull field and then we were there. We stayed for tea then tried to get a bus but it just sailed past so we had to walk a mile to the station.

The train came in packed. People were going in the guard's van, so we got in with them. There were quite a few bicycles in the van so Mart-boy [Bridget's little brother] and I sat on them. There were about twenty people in the guard's van, with the temperature at ninety.

At Chalfont we left about fifty or more people behind and at Chorleywood about ten people managed to get on.

At Rickmansworth a few people got off and at Moor Park and Sandy Lodge a few more got off. After Moor Park we went straight through to Harrow, where a lot of people got off, but as the train went on to Wembley Park we stayed on it. We got home feeling perfectly baked. In spite of all the crush we enjoyed ourselves and it was nice to get away from the air raids.

What to do with pets was a problem facing holiday-goers and stay-at-homes alike. Many domestic cats and dogs had been put to sleep for fear they would be killed or injured in bombing raids or gas attacks. The government was also worried that people would share their rations with their pets and as a result be undernourished themselves (with the knock-on effect that an undernourished population would be less able to stand out against the enemy); or that, unable to feed their animals, they would turn them out on to the streets to starve. The official line taken by the National Air Raid Precautions Animals Committee was that if you couldn't care for your pet yourself or leave it with neighbours, it was kinder to have it destroyed.

Rose's family was one of the lucky ones: they *were* able to care for their dog, Bob. In June 1940, Rose wrote to her sister:

We had to think about where we should go for our holiday. Mum is absolutely desperate to go somewhere, I have never seen her so set on it before. Usually, in other years, if Dad had said we could not have gone she would have said, 'All right, then, we'll stop at home.' But not this year, so she promptly sat down and wrote to Mrs West at Newquay, asking if she could put the three of us up. Dad of course will stay where he is. Then of course I did not think the long train journey to Newquay would be any good for Bob. Not like a car journey where he could get out every couple of hours or so. [So after lunch] Chris took Mum and Lil and I and the dog to the Shooters Hill kennels. They charge a shilling a day. They have 140 dogs in quarantine, and 130 boarders and some in the Hospital. We had a look round, and think we will have to leave him there for a fortnight. All the dogs seemed full of life and health, but I noticed one little blackie very sorrowful and sad. His people had gone for a fortnight and I expect he missed them.

There is no account of that holiday in Rose's letters to her sister, but it was presumeably a success, because in August she reported:

> I have sent a box of peaches to the Wests at Newquay. We have not had so many this year and they are on the small side, but they are 1/3 each in the shops, so we have eaten a few £s worth. Unfortunately, no more cream is going to be made or sold after October 1st, so we shall be creamless.

The following summer saw them in Devon:

> We had quite a nice lazy time at Sidmouth; the weather was very hot the first week, but showery the second. It is quite a small place so it did not tempt us to take much exercise anyway, and mostly we lounged about in the lounge which overlooked the sea, or just on the front. Going down we lost our way a bit and so gradually got on another road, but we had a very pretty run, although a long one eventually, and were very tired when we arrived. Coming home we came another route, and it poured with rain the whole time. We put Bob in the usual kennels, but goodness knows what they fed him on, he had a terrible time when he came home. When he gets upset, like when he is lost, his innards go all funny, but this time it was terrible, and he was bad for a week before he gradually got all right again, although I don't really think he is very well, his nose is more often than

not hot. He went nearly crazy when he was collected, in the car and when he came home, and it took him a long time to calm down.

Bob survived that particular ordeal; another year later, in June 1942, Rose was able to report:

Well, we are now back after a very nice holiday. I hope sometime when you come to England you will have a little holiday at little Switzerland. The scenery is lovely where we went and is an ideal place for hikers and young people to roam about. We of course did not do much walking, but Mum one day took quite a long walk with us along the glen and the tumbling water amid the leafy foliage. Of course she was pretty tired when she got back, but we stopped an hour for tea and had a rest in a valley surrounded by big hills. Bob enjoyed himself immensely, but the poor little devil wanted crutches after a couple of days, climbing either up- or downhill. Hilly places are of course very beautiful in scenery, but I am afraid are rather hard on poor legs, animal, vegetable and the rest. He used to plod wearily about, and although he was very tired, he wouldn't be left behind. When we got to the gate he used to stand there watching us, with his head cocked on one side, debating whether to go any further. Anyway, I think he enjoyed his holiday.

Joan sometimes travelled from Northamptonshire to London on her own, and the family dog featured in her story, too:

I was put on the train in the care of the guard and my instructions were, when I got to Euston, I was to stay on the platform until the dog found me. My aunt's dog, Paddy. She used to let him off his leash and he'd come and find me. He was a cocker spaniel and he was a war baby. My uncle and his brothers had a carpentry business and they were kept busy shoring up houses that had been bombed. He went home one day with this puppy in his pocket. They'd been working on a house and a lady came along and asked if someone would take the pup. She bred cocker spaniels and out of two litters she had one baby left. She had nowhere to live because her house had been flattened. So Uncle took the puppy home.

Usually when I went back to Northamptonshire, my aunt and sometimes my uncle too would take me, and they'd bring the dog, on the train. Behind where we were living there were fields. Before we went, Auntie always used to insist that we bath him, but I don't know why, because the minute we got there he was out the door, rolling in cow pats. And then my mother would be standing at the door and saying, 'I'm not having him back in here till he's clean.' Oh, we had some fun. Yes, it was wartime, but luckily, with the family that I've got, they made it fun.

Children who remained in London found new recreation grounds. Sheila was in Stepney:

We weren't far from the docks, which were always being bombed, and there were big warehouses that the Germans wanted to get rid of – to stop all the goods coming in. When there were raids we used to go down into the underground station, but one night later in the war for some reason we didn't get there and Mum, my brother and I were under the stairs. It was the time of the doodlebugs, and we could hear them coming over, making that awful vroom, vroom, vroom noise, and then it stopped very close by and we thought, 'Oh no, where's it going to hit?' Our street got it that night, the whole house was shaking. We were OK when we came out, but a lot of the street wasn't. There was a public house on the corner and two houses next to the pub were completed flattened; then there were two more houses and then our house, so that was a close call.

The bombsites were our playground, so you can imagine we had plenty of them to play in. We used to make camps – pile the bricks and rubble up to make seats, take our sandwiches or an apple in there and eat them. We made homes out of them and had great fun, to be honest. But I remember going shopping with my mum the morning after a raid and various women would be standing around chatting and asking, 'Who got it last night?' 'Oh, so-and-so street.' 'How many gone?' That's how it was. It was awful, but it was our way of life.

Shirley was at primary school in South London, where bombsites were all around:

> We were very phlegmatic. My mother would have been horrified to know that we played on bombsites on our way back from school, but we did. One day a policeman came and said, 'You're not taking anything off this bombsite, are you?'
>
> 'No, no,' we lied. We'd found some paper, which we knew was a real luxury. Paper and books were very scarce. Envelopes used to be used again and again and again until there was no space to write another address. But the policeman absolutely terrified us. We burst into tears and said we were sorry.

By the end of the war Shirley had moved to secondary school in Hammersmith, West London:

> I remember playing tennis at school in the summer, but we couldn't play cricket because the RAF had taken over the cricket pitch and there was what looked like a silver whale in the sky above it – a barrage balloon.

Barrage balloons were designed to make bombers fly higher, where they were more vulnerable to anti-aircraft fire. Anne has a strange memory of them:

> At the end of our garden we had a barrage balloon – huge, like an elephant. It was silvery grey and I think it

even had ears: it really did look like an elephant in the sky. It swayed in the wind and it made a funny noise: to me as a little girl it definitely seemed like a living being.

CHAPTER 8

'JUST CAMPING OUT IN RATHER A NOISY BIT OF COUNTRY'

The United States had entered the Second World War after the Japanese bombed Pearl Harbor in December 1941. Shortly afterwards, American soldiers – eventually a total of over a million and a half of them – appeared in Britain and joined the preparations for Allied assaults on Europe.

These Americans were about as unlike wartime Britons as it was possible to be, and their commanders knew it. Guidelines issued to help the newcomers become better 'acquainted with the British, their country, and their ways' included the warning that British reserve should not be mistaken for unfriendliness; that for all their politeness the British were tough; and that Americans invited into British homes should be careful not to eat too much, lest they consume the family's rations for a week. They might find everything about Britain (including, perhaps, its people) a bit grimy and grey, but they should remember that there had been a war on since 1939.

To British children in particular, the Americans were the source of previously unimagined treats. They had access to all sorts of luxuries, and their generosity often seemed, to the deprived British, more like wanton extravagance.

Brenda in Enham, Hampshire, remembers:

The Americans used to drive through the village quite often and just throw out packets of nylons and things like that. I can remember people running behind the lorries and picking things up. A cousin of mine lived in Andover and her husband told a similar story: the Americans used to go through on the train and they were given lots of food packets, but it seemed as if all they ever wanted was the chewing gum. After they'd taken the gum they used to chuck everything else out the window. Of course everyone was very poor during the war, with not a lot of food, and a gang of lads would go down the railway track, picking up these food packets, because they came in handy, obviously.

John recalls similar experiences when the American fleet was stationed in Weymouth Bay:

The Americans were so well looked after, so well off compared with the Brits. They were issued with things called K rations, which were boxes of what they regarded as 'essentials'. But I think they just took out the cigarettes, the chewing gum and one or two other things; the rest they tossed overboard and it came floating ashore. We could go along the beach and pick up whatever we found. We discovered some funny stuff in packets that turned out to be powdered coffee. It was our first introduction to instant coffee – in fact, I think it was my first introduction to coffee of any kind.

Audrey was also in Weymouth and remembers a particular incidence of the Americans' generosity:

There was one time my father took the dog out for a walk and he came back with a big paper bag full of doughnuts – ring doughnuts, with lots of sugar and lots of jam. I don't know how it happened, but he must have met an American. They always seemed to have plenty of everything. So we were given all these doughnuts, which we passed round to everybody.

What John calls 'the Americans' freewheeling approach' provided a new summer activity:

Their troops were issued with inflatable life jackets in the form of two cloth-coated rubber tubes about three feet long. Several of these were washed up on the beaches inside Portland Harbour. Presumably it was too much trouble to retrieve them after life-saving practice. Two joined together made a raft like a lilo, and we managed to assemble a small fleet which we used for mock battles

or as swimming aids long after the Yanks had left to do
their bit on the Continent.

That 'bit on the Continent' came in June 1944 and was
one of the most significant events of the entire war – the
landing of some 150,000 troops, primarily British, Canadian
and American, on the beaches of Normandy. They were
supported by 7,000 sailing craft and 12,000 aircraft in an
offensive known as the D-Day Landings, or simply D-Day.

June in Andover remembers being aware of the build-up
for some time:

> For months we had been used to the heavy drone of
> bombers overhead once again. This time they were ours
> on the way to targets in Germany. A ban on eastern and
> southern coastal zones, stretching from King's Lynn in
> Norfolk all the way round to Newquay in Cornwall, was
> declared in March. Andover was only five miles north
> of the quite broad banned area, and suffered from the
> severe restrictions on travel into it. Only people with
> important business or strong personal reasons could
> obtain the necessary permits. Some through routes were
> closed, one of these being the road to Winchester from
> just beyond Wherwell. Stories filtered back to the town
> that the tree-lined verges of that road were packed with
> army vehicles.

Mervyn from Gloucestershire, in his mid-teens by this time,
also witnessed the preparations:

For many months in late '43 and early '44 the skies of Gloucestershire were filled with training aircraft and also with others towing gliders. Late on the evening of 2 June 1944, there was a continuous roar in the sky and we went outside to see a stream of tugs and gliders, three abreast and with lights on. No aircraft had shown lights since 1939. This stream of aircraft went on for around three hours. The same happened the following evening. Poor weather obviously prevented a repeat on the next night, then on the night of the 5th, it all happened again. We woke the next morning to the news that the Normandy landings had started. We had witnessed the rehearsals for D-Day.

In May of that year we had seen that the American Ambulance Unit, based nearby in Wotton-under-Edge and Dursley, had adjusted the exhausts of their vehicles so that they discharged above the cab and had smeared the engines with copious amounts of grease. When I arrived at school one morning the town was so quiet – the Americans had gone overnight. They too would soon be in France.

Alex, who described himself as a 'very young soldier', was serving in South London:

From Woolwich Common, high above the Thames, the pre-dawn still had been drowned with the drone of many hundreds of British and Allied bombers, on their way to 'soften-up' the firmly entrenched German Army of Occupation in France.

We all more than guessed it was D-Day Dawn; for several weeks we had seen the massing of troops and equipment moving into Kent and the grapevine told of landing-craft loaded with Allied Armies, waiting in harbours and estuaries along the south coast, for the rough weather to clear.

As the sun rose that sparklingly clear summer morning, all of our Fire Platoon at the Royal Military Repository, Woolwich Common, were outside at the best vantage points, sky-watching to catch the first glimpses of the air armada heading out, over Central London, eastwards, or rather south-eastwards towards France.

There was a lull which started just as the first rays of light broke the horizon. A few tardy bombers, perhaps, trying to catch up with the main force, caught the first sunlight and, in spite of the dull camouflage paint, glowed as if on fire.

We had started to return to the billet hut, thinking that we had missed the main show. The air was still and silent with little hint of the drama to come. Being young (and stupid) and sensing that there was more to come, I had dawdled behind the others and was still at the iron railings that separated the military property from the public road and the expanse of Woolwich Common beyond.

Then, quite suddenly, the sky above the horizon was filled with dots, like a huge widespread flock of homeward-bound crows on a summer's evening. It was a while before they came close enough to make out silhouettes – most of us were pretty skilled at aircraft recognition in those days, when life might pivot on the knowing of a Messerschmitt 109 fighter from a Hurricane or a Spitfire; or being able to tell a Messerschmitt 110 fighter-bomber from a British Mosquito; or the German Junkers Ju 88 from a Bristol Blenheim bomber.

Then, when they were somewhere above Central London, with Saint Paul's dome and twin shining, as if so proud that England was at last striking back at the grey-clad, half-million strong German Seventh Army. The thrill of excitement that ran through me, as I stood alone, for a little while, watching approaching aircraft, that surely and steadily carried the airborne troops that were to drop behind the Normandy beaches and have such a crucial bearing on the successes of that day... Tuesday, the Sixth of June, Nineteen Forty-Four.

So, from the vantage point of Woolwich Common, we watched the hundreds of airplanes, some singly, some towing the 'Hamilcar' troop and equipment transporting gliders, all marked with the three white and intervening two black stripes on each wing and on the fuselage that were to identify the Allied aircraft from those of the enemy.

It is hard, now, to really accept what we saw. Aircraft spread from [a bit] to the south [to] as far as we could clearly see to the north. The width of the 'flock' was at least ten miles wide and it took at least a quarter of an hour to fly overhead. Even if the separation was a hundred yards between aircraft, there must have been close to two hundred aircraft abreast; if they flew at 150 miles per hour and each 'flock' was half a mile apart, the figure of about seventy-five 'wings' is suggested, 200 x 150? One thousand bomber raids had become common, by the Allies over Occupied Europe – but thirty thousand? No, it could not have been, although it certainly looked like it that morning.

Barbara, working as a Land Girl in Sussex, remembers the big change that D-Day brought:

Two days or so before D-Day we had come into Hastings to go to the pictures and there was a strange sort of silence about the place. Normally there was quite a noise with many servicemen about, but on this occasion the town was almost deserted. Leaving Crowhurst for work one morning just after this, we looked towards the sea and there were all these vessels, including some very oddly shaped ones, moving down the Channel. We guessed then why Hastings had suddenly emptied – D-Day had come!

The build-up in the Weymouth area was extraordinary, as John recalls:

In order to get to school, I had to go down a hill known as Boot Hill. To reach the beach where the Americans had set up temporary accommodation, on the edge of Portland, they had to come up Boot Hill and one day three or four of us on our bikes were stopped there for an hour and a half while a non-stop convoy of the troops went past, on their way to set up camp. As D-Day drew nearer and nearer, the whole harbour became full of landing craft; the area above it, above Chesil Beach, was just continuous canvas, where they had their camp.

But although they were preparing for a massive military operation, there was very little security. One weekend we did our usual walk along the cliffs, just to watch the waves coming in over Chesil Beach, which was always a spectacular sight, and there was no restriction on walking through the American lines. I was able to talk to the man who had been left in charge of the camp while the others were having some time off in the town. I remember it clearly, because I think it was the first time I had seen a black man close up and it was certainly the first time I had spoken to one.

By the time they were ready, there were so many ships in Portland Harbour and in Weymouth Bay that you could literally have walked across the bay from one side to the other – they were all lined up, just a few feet apart. Then one morning we woke up and they were gone. The harbour was empty – it was extraordinary; literally an overnight transformation and suddenly we had our harbour back. Once the Americans had gone we could get back to playing on the beach; it wasn't long before the anti-tank defence was dismantled.

Sub-lieutenant Jimmy Green of the Royal Navy was twenty-two years old and in charge of a landing craft that took American troops into one of the Normandy beaches:

We were called the suicide wave, the first ones to go in. Our landing craft were lowered from a larger troop ship and into the sea about 15 miles from Omaha Beach. It was pitch-black and blowing a gale. I suppose I was scared, but I was more concerned with getting all my boats in on time for H-hour [the hour when the operation was due to begin]. Aged 22, I didn't think anything would happen to me. All the British crew were quite relaxed – we chatted among ourselves. The American soldiers we were taking in were apprehensive. They'd never faced enemy fire before. Nor were they used to the rough conditions and some of them were being sea-sick. We really bashed into the waves as we tried to keep up our speed. We were taking a lot of sea spray...

We went full speed towards the beach and when we hit bottom I released the ramp. There was an eerie silence, just the wind and the waves. The Germans must just have been watching us. I think we were the very first to land in Occupied France.

The Americans were very grim-faced, but filed out with no hesitation into the water – which in some places was up to their knees, and up to their shoulders in others. My job was finished. I'd taken them to the beach. Their job had only just begun.

Just along the coast at Gold Beach, Lieutenant L E Anderson also had a choppy landing:

> D-Day 7.30 a.m. An assault craft heading for Gold Beach with some of my signallers and myself with a Naval Boatswain. The rule was that, as long as we were at sea, the Boatswain was in charge, but I was in command as soon as we touched the shore. We ended up on an underwater obstacle sticking up through the bottom of the boat, which made it spin like a roulette wheel in the rough sea. There then ensued what seemed to be a lengthy discussion between the Boatswain and myself as to whether we were at sea or shore. Ultimately, I won and he let down the ramp. With the famous cry of 'Follow me, chaps', I ran off the ramp to find myself up to my neck in water.

Gordon, a member of the Canadian Regina Rifles, remembers his regiment's landing on Juno Beach:

> So far, not a shot has been fired from the defenders on the beach. Will it be a push-over? We soon have the answer in the form of machine-gun fire and shells from pillboxes which are apparently still open for business despite the terrific pounding they have taken.

The Canadian Scots Regiment came ashore at nine o'clock in the morning, meeting 'scattered resistance' behind the beaches. Then they struck inland. One of the regiment remembers:

A German 88-mm gun, camouflaged in a hay stack, began firing and destroying vehicles as they moved off the beach. Major Plows, commanding officer for 'A' Company, ordered Lieutenant Bernie Clarke's platoon to take out the dangerous gun emplacement. Clarke's classic reply was 'Who? Me?', and he immediately set out to clear up the spot. They crawled up a knoll to within 75 yards of the position, nabbed several Germans, and then raced in… A door leading into the emplacement was pulled open and someone threw in a grenade. That did the trick. So quick and sudden was the Canadian action that about fifty German soldiers came out of their slit trenches – all surrendering. It was at this point that 'A' Company's second in command, Captain William H.V. Matthews, came running up, asking Clarke, 'What the hell are you trying to do, win the VC?'

For many, the landings were just the beginning of the story. Michael was an officer in the Royal Tank Regiment. On 13 June 1944 he wrote to his mother from Normandy:

You asked in one of your letters whether one ever gets used to the noise of battle; the answer is definitely 'yes', in the same way as one becomes used to the noise of traffic in a busy town. Sometimes a particularly heavy outburst of firing from our own artillery is a bit disturbing but only if the guns are very near, i.e. within quarter of a mile. Of course enemy shells are still disturbing but not so much so as they were at first. Also one attains a sort of protective armour against the shock of seeing and hearing of one's friends being killed and wounded. Fortunately, only one of the officers in my squadron has been wounded and he is now back in England. ...

I will now summarise the sort of life we are living as best I can:

Number of times we have been inside a building since landing: Never

Times we have had bread: Once

Entertainment: Nil

Times we have had beer: Never

Whisky and gin: Several times

Fresh meat: Once...a captured chicken!

Fresh potatoes: Several times...found in abandoned fields

Fresh food of any other kind: Never

Newspapers: Often, sometimes only two days old

Bath: Never

Seen a N.A.A.F.I. or Café in any sort of working order: Never

Do we get enough sleep? Plenty

Do we get enough to eat? Plenty

Are we quite happy and content: Definitely (I am at any rate)

Are we winning the war? Undoubtedly yes

Do I love my family more than I can say? I certainly do.

It wasn't all as cheerful as that, though. On 30 June, Michael wrote again:

Well, now to discuss the last 4 days. The first was our battle innoculation and we had no casualties in our squadron whatsoever. At first I was thoroughly enjoying it all and no one seemed at all nervous, then I saw some of our infantry killed by a mortar and suddenly realised that this was not just a game. But we met no anti-tank guns and so had no scares at all. The second evening we ran into real trouble in a village and sustained our first casualties. Fear for my own safety was almost nil, but anxiety for our squadron was intense, and when a tank containing one of our officers went up in flames, tears tried hard to flow but I managed to hold them back. Actually, our casualties were light, but being our first shook us a lot at first.

And on 12 July:

Well, we had a hell of a battle on Monday. We moved up to our positions at 3 a.m. and went into battle at 5 a.m. We were in all day with only about 1 hour in all out of the tank until 11.30 at night, 20 hours on end. You can imagine how we slept afterwards.

Yesterday we rested and refitted with only a few shells quite a distance away to bother us although we are only just out of the line. We are rather hoping for a real rest now out of shellfire and away from the noise of battle for the first time since 26th June. We saw 4 Jerry planes shot down in about 5 mins yesterday by A.A. guns.

The other great delight was a bread issue, quarter of a loaf per man, the first since we landed. We are still resting now and feeling very fit and well. I am so used to sleeping under my tank that anywhere else will feel quite queer. It is a wonderful bomb-proof, shell-proof bedroom and is just right for the five of us.

15 July:

You must remember that the actual fighting is a very small part of our lives (though all important), and most of the time we are just camping out in rather a noisy bit of country. At present we are back resting, not right back, but far enough for safety. We have a wireless with a loud-speaker and yesterday we had a show by an army concert party; it was very good, too.

We have had no bread since that once on Tuesday, but we are hoping for some beer, a quart per man is on the way up! So we are leading a life of ease which before the war people would have travelled miles for.

A few Jerry planes were over yesterday. They did not molest us but were given the most colossal A. A. reception and nipped off pretty quickly, losing one on the way. Now I am sitting on an empty ammunition box using a map case on a petrol can as a table, waiting for a nice hot meal of bully beef and new potatoes. The weather has been good for a long time now and instead of complaining of mud, we are now complaining of dust. We are never satisfied, are we!

23 July:

...Now I will end by describing our first air raid. We moved up to relieve another Battalion just behind the front line at about 10 p.m. Just as it got dark, a few motors came over and their ferocious bark soon sent us to hole below the tanks. At about 11.15, three planes flew over very low; they were apparently Junkers 88s. They circled back and dropped parachute flares, lighting everything up and making us feel a bit naked and then hell was let loose; they zoomed down and let fly sticks of bombs just below our Battalion H.Q. tanks. We heard only a slight whistle and then enormous explosions, four at a time in quick succession; the ground shook and we lay huddled in our hole, very frightened at this new experience but no-one showed it outwardly and we couldn't see one another's expressions in the dark. Just as we were recovering from this the dose was repeated, crash – crash – crash – crash. It was a horrible experience; but a necessary one as we now know what little harm it does us and were not nearly so frightened when it happened again the following night.

When the bombers had gone the mortars bombarded us intermittently for about an hour, but did no damage at all. Nonetheless it was the most horrible night I have ever experienced. Since then mortaring and shelling happens quite frequently, but hardly ever hurts us and no longer frightens us unless we are in the open. Even then you nearly always hear the swish through the air and quickly dive under a tank or into a ditch.

This effect is quite interesting as we constantly shell the Boche at least fifty times as heavily as he does us (this is no exaggeration), and it must be ghastly.

On 26 July, Michael was promoted to the rank of major and on the same day, two of his troop officers were killed. He described this as 'a new horror for us and found us quite unprepared':

Emotionally, I have never before been so badly hurt; but I think I have now endured every kind of emotional upset bar bailing out of a knocked-out tank; and this I hope never to do. War is an appalling thing; I never realised before quite how horrible it was and we all long for it to be over...

I read a letter taken off a dead German and circulated to us in English; he said 'better 2 years in Russia than one day in Normandy'. They certainly are getting appalling casualties, shelled and bombed day and night and periodically being slaughtered by devastating offences by the Allies. The effect is definitely noticeable in the numbers who surrender now, compared with the few who did at first.

Michael was right to be optimistic, but not from a personal point of view: he was killed in early 1945 after a mortar shell hit the top of his tank. A comrade's letter of condolence to Michael's parents said, 'He died as he always said he hoped he would if he had to, leading the Squadron and without knowing it has happened.'

D-Day may have been hailed a great Allied victory, but it brought many tragedies too. At least 2,500 Allied troops were killed and three times that number wounded. Irvine, aged fourteen by this time, remembers:

As the war dragged on a Canadian cousin called in to see Grandma and Granddad. It was towards the end of May 1944. Walter was in his twenties and a fighter pilot in the Royal Canadian Air Force. There was a lot of excited talk about beating the Germans. To everyone's delight, especially Granddad's, he stayed several days and said he would come again.

His home was in Alberta and he flew an American Mustang fighter plane, which, when powered by a Rolls-Royce Merlin engine, became one of the best all-round Allied fighter planes in the entire war. Loyally, Walter had hoped to fly the famous Spitfire, if only to take part in one aerial battle. He was an enthusiastic, likeable man.

A few days later, on 6 June, Allied troops began landing on the beaches of Normandy. It was the long-awaited D-Day and the battle to free Europe began. In the days that followed Cousin Walter was among the thousands of members of the Allied forces who were killed.

John from Weymouth, Dorset, has a memory from much later in life:

Many years after the war my wife and I were visiting an old colleague of mine who had retired to Cornwall. It happened to be 6 June – the anniversary of D-Day – so I asked Tony where he had been on that day in 1944. He was several years older than me, came from another part of the country and we hadn't known each other then, so it was a complete coincidence that he said, 'I was in Weymouth Bay.' A nineteen-year-old subaltern in the Horse Guards, he'd been on the extreme right-hand side of the British fleet of tank-landing craft. He and his troops were sitting having a drink and a bit of a laugh. Right next to him was the first of the American landing craft, just a few feet away. Tony called over to his American counterpart and said, 'You're not having much fun.'

The American agreed, 'No, we're not having much fun. Have you done this before?'

'No,' Tony replied, 'this is our first time', to which the American responded, 'You won't be laughing this time tomorrow, boy.'

All those years later, Tony said to me, 'He was quite right.' They went over on D-2, the second day of the invasion, and about 20 per cent of his troops didn't make it. He didn't talk much about the war.

Margaret's fiancé Geoff was one of the lucky ones, but he wasn't unscathed:

He was in the parachute regiment and he went over on the first day. His battalion had to attack the Merville battery, the famous battery that needed to be silenced at the very beginning of the invasion, before the other troops landed. So that was pretty hairy. That was in June and he was wounded in the August, quite badly wounded, and flown home and then discharged from the army after that. So he was really very lucky.

We didn't hear for ages from the War Office what had happened to him. I heard first of all from the Women's Voluntary Service, as it then was. After being flown home, he was sent by train to South Wales; the WVS met the trains and gave the wounded a card, which they wrote on, and Geoff's card was sent to us. That was the first intimation I had that anything had happened to him. It wasn't until weeks after that that we heard formally from the War Office. The numbers of wounded were so great that they weren't able to keep up with it. By that time I'd actually been down to Wales to visit him, having to stand all the way on the train. But he survived, so he was luckier than many.

His unit had been in a wood surrounded by an SS battalion or something and they were ordered to break out. That's when he was wounded. He never really talked about it until we started going back to France for holidays, years later, and went to some of the places he had been. That was when he told me about being strapped to the bonnet of a jeep and driven to the field hospital. He'd never seemed to want to talk about it before then. I think people didn't, when they'd been through so much.

Among the Canadian forces were members of the Royal Winnipeg Rifles regiment, whose history of the landings on Juno Beach contain this horrifying story:

Rushing the enemy, 'B' Company encountered heavy enemy fire. Corporal Klos, badly shot in the stomach and legs while leaving the assault boat, made his way forward to an enemy machine-gun nest. He managed to kill two Nazis before he was mortally felled. His hands still gripped about the throat of his victim produced a chilling sight!

If Margaret's fiancé's experiences were anything like that, it's small wonder he hadn't wanted to talk about them.

CHAPTER 9

'JUST AS WE WERE THINKING IT WAS ALL OVER, IT WAS BACK TO SQUARE ONE'

An offensive as huge as the D-Day Landings was always likely to provoke a retaliation, and it did. The German response came a mere week later.

After the excitement of D-Day, Alex in Woolwich, South-East London, reported that the next few days 'were something of an anti-climax':

We had all expected the Luftwaffe to mount a massive reprisal raid on London and had steeled ourselves for air attack.

D-Day Plus One came and went. We listened intently to BBC Radio News, but, although it gave constantly encouraging news, little actual detail.

D-Day Plus Two was much the same. We would strain our ears and imagine we could heard the sounds of gunfire 125 miles – 200 km – to the south of us, but, of course, we could not.

D-Day Plus Three and we saw the military ambulances bring the casualties back to the Herbert Military Hospital, just further up the Common.

D-Day Plus Four. There was more news coming through, the Saturday papers gave more maps and arrows showing the trends of the attack and told of successes – and of 'stiff resistance'.

D-Day Plus Five, Sunday, and I think that most of Britain went to church to pray for the Boys in France.

Those who were expecting something to happen didn't have much longer to wait. The first of the V1 – doodlebug – flying bombs struck the East End of London in the early hours of D-Day Plus Seven, 13 June. Two nights later, Alex was woken by the sirens:

There were no searchlights to be seen, not like the pre-dawn attack two days before, it was dark and we needed torches to see and avoid obstructions in the Black-out.

We readied the fire-pump for action, checking fuel levels, hoses, fittings and tools; but before we had completed this task, quick as it was, we could hear the distant rattle of gun-fire…The ack-ack barrage was intense and growing louder and even more intense by the second.

We had all grown used to the strum-strum-strum sound of the approaching German bombers and we could nearly always tell the 'Jerry' from the sound of 'our' bombers.

But there was a new sound emerging from the rattle of the nearing gun-fire, the same sound we had heard the morning of the single flying-bomb attack – the rapid putt-putt-putt-putt of some new sort of engine.

This time the new sound was not being drowned out by the noise of the ack-ack; that night the putt-putt-putting was drowning out the noise of the gunfire. We turned off the light and opened the double doors; although it was from behind us, as we faced the opened doors, the new sound was already frighteningly loud.

Suddenly the 3.7-inch guns on the Common close by opened fire, again with an unusual sound, which we soon realised, as the guns swung around and fired low over the buildings that surrounded us and the shells whined overhead, because the 3.7 guns were firing at very low elevation, not like we had always heard them before, firing almost straight up into the sky.

Then the new noise was overhead, punctuated by the occasional whoof-boom of heavy bombs exploding, some near, but many further away.

Unable to contend with curiosity some of us took a few paces outside of the concrete-roof shelter, looking up to see the cause of the new sound.

But there was nothing to see but low cloud glowing in an odd light of flashes from the guns and exploding shells, as some Faustic thunderstorm was raging. This strange putt-putt-putting was overhead and far away to our left and right, the noise was coming from a dozen points overhead, then one by one the sounds ceased – just as though the source of the sound had suddenly disappeared.

Shrapnel, big lumps, suddenly came raining down on the yard about us and on corrugated-iron roofs of the workshops about us. We dived for cover and, for just an instant, forgot about the sound.

Then there was a brilliant flash; all of us hit the floor, reacting to experience, we hung on to the rims of our steel helmets and waited for the bang and the blast.

The bang came, loud and close, but not the blast; there had been no screaming howl, like any other falling bomb makes, from a near miss, as that one surely was. The building rattled and shattered glass smashed not so far away.

I still remember thinking – what sort of bomb is that, that has such a wallop yet so little blast?

The ack-ack barrage was suddenly stopping, as if all the guns had run out of ammunition.

Most of the putt-putt-putt sound had gone, too, replaced by the crash of bombs falling away over towards the City of London.

Then there was silence for a few minutes. The 'all-clear' steady wail of the siren sounded and, still in shocked silence, we shut the fire-pump in and headed for bed again.

Not five minutes after the all-clear, the sirens wailed out their banshee 'Warning'.

A flight of low-flying night-fighters flew out from the

Hendon direction and headed off from whence the last attack had originated.

No sooner back at fire-station when the even deeper and more concentrated sound of ack-ack fire came to our ears.

Closer at hand, a fire-engine, bell clanging, hurried to some 'incident', heading out from Sunbury Street, Woolwich, in the direction of Greenwich. Then, again, the whole performance repeated itself and the attack was over in a few minutes.

The all-clear sounded and again we set off towards our beds, treading upon ack-ack shell fragments as we returned.

Back at the hut, the off-duty men of the Fire Platoon were either sitting and smoking around the unlit stove, or sitting up in bed, pallid and silent.

In London, amongst the 'Squaddies', there was an unwritten 'rule' that even in the worst of air raids, it was 'yellow' to go to the air-raid shelter. The fellow in the next bed to mine asked: 'Wot's up, Alec?'

'Hitler's secret weapon, I reckon.'

I'd expected someone to scoff at the suggestion, but there was silence, tacit acceptance, at last, that I had been right in my interpretation of what the newspapers had been warning us of.

Then the siren sounded again. I looked at my wrist-watch and saw that, again, a quarter of an hour had elapsed since the last warning.

While Alex was in Woolwich, Jim was working as a trainee

fireman not five miles away and almost certainly witnessed the same attack:

At about six o'clock on this beautiful midsummer morning I came off duty to walk home in that special light that only June can create. I was feeling a little lonely as I walked homeward bound along Blackheath Road, when suddenly I could hear that horrific sound in the distance. Looking in the direction that it was coming from, I could see a fiery light in the cloudless sky, so I stopped as it got closer. It was coming in my direction and would pass at about thirty degrees from going overhead. As it quickly got closer, I could see that it was shaped like a crude aircraft with a jet of orange flame trailing from the rear. My eyes were glued to this strange black object that sounded like a powerful motorbike without a silencer. That was exactly what it should have sounded like, for that was the way it had been deliberately designed, right down to that orange flame. A Spitfire appeared to be in hot pursuit but, in reality, the Spitfire had been overtaken by what was to be known as the V1 rocket. Eventually the secret weapon flew out of sight with the Spitfire losing the apparent chase. For some unknown reason I wasn't afraid, but I was puzzled and eager to get home, hoping that neither Mum, Ivy or Bert had witnessed the awesome sight that I wished to describe.

Roy in Ealing, West London, approaching his fourteenth

birthday, remembers a feeling of optimism immediately after D-Day: 'Could this really be the beginning of the end?' But a week or so later:

I was out with my friend Ken after school when the air-raid sirens sounded. 'What's that all about? Must be a mistake.' Surely Jerry was far too busy to make some r andom attack on London. 'Ignore it, it will go away.' It did, the all-clear sounded.

'Told you so, some silly bugger pressed the wrong button.'

A few minutes later we were not so sure, the alert sounded again. What was going on?

So it continued for the rest of that day. Alternating warnings and the all-clear. No planes, no gunfire. No nothing.

This was getting silly. Rumours were rife. Some people reckoned that they had heard explosions in the distance. Others had heard that 'Jerry' was sending over silent planes.

A more plausible theory was that they were shelling London with a huge long-range gun on the French coast but, if that was so, how did they know when to sound the sirens?

Nothing made sense and it became increasingly obvious that there was some form of a news black-out. This only added to the wild speculation.

The pattern continued the following day. We were up and down the school shelters like yo-yos. After school I met up with Ken about a mile from home. The sirens sounded yet again, but we ignored them.

Suddenly, our activities were interrupted by a strange, deep-throated pulsating drone that increased in volume until a small aircraft hurtled into view, travelling very fast and low.

'What the hell is that!' we both exclaimed. 'The tail's on fire.' Questions tumbled. 'What's the pipe thing on top?'

It hurtled over and disappeared from view as we stood totally bewildered, listening to the receding sound like a heavily laden motor bike chugging uphill. 'It's stopped!' What now?

Seconds elapsed, then 'whooph' came the sound of a distant explosion.

We had just witnessed the first of many V1 Flying Bombs to reach the western suburbs. Updated rumours now came thick and fast. They are pilotless planes was the popular opinion. Not so far from the truth, really. Suicide pilots was another version.

As more and more came over the sirens were sounding constantly. On one day there were seventeen separate warnings, which caused total confusion.

Our cellar shelter regained all the old regulars. Just as we were thinking it was all over, it was back to square one.

Wendy, aged eleven, recalls that the new bombs were frightening:

In June 1944, I was off school, recovering from

rheumatic fever. I recall several times when my mother and I stood in the kitchen hearing the drone of a doodlebug. The moment the drone stopped we started counting. I don't remember how long we had to continue before we knew we were safe from the attack, but they were nerve-racking moments.

Brenda in Swanley, Kent, also remembers being scared for the first time:

By that time I was ten, so I suppose I was old enough to understand. The houses opposite were bombed – the bombs often came up over our house and I do remember that awful feeling when the noise stopped and you wondered where they were going to land. The ceiling came down in our house one night and the windows were blown out, but the council came round the next morning and put them back. We lived on an estate near Swanley station, and of course stations were always a target. I can remember being afraid of that.

Bridget was nine:

It was mostly when I was woken in the night with air raids and I suppose it was our guns going off, and we'd have to go out into the shelter – that was horrible. But I don't know what I was frightened of. I don't think I had a picture of what might happen; I don't think I thought a German was coming to get me – it just wasn't nice, being woken up by loud noises in the middle of the night. If a flying bomb came over when we were on the train to school, it would stop, the guard would open his door and look out and then on we'd go again. I don't remember ever thinking, 'I won't be going home' or even that when I got home something might have happened to the house. I wasn't frightened in that way.

In a letter to her sister written at the time, she describes an early-morning raid – and gives an interesting insight into a nine-year-old's priorities. GOP stands for *Girl's Own Paper*, a popular comic which was a precious commodity in these times of paper shortage:

At about 6.30 a warning went and at 7 a doodlebug went over. As we were in bed, we did not care much. At 8 the raid was still on, and as we were having breakfast, we heard one coming. We dashed out to the shelter and I yelled out to Daddy to tell me when he could see it. Just then he pointed up into the sky and shouted, 'There it is.' We went out into the garden, it looked simply lovely, all silvery with a blaze at the end, even Mummy thought so. All at once the blaze went out and we heard the engines stop. It glided for a bit, then dropped, but we did not hear it bang.

With lots of love

Bridget

PS I am enclosing August GOP.

Ros in Surrey suffered a near miss:

When the doodlebugs came, I was fifteen and due to leave school soon. One glorious summer day I was supposed to go for an interview with the *News Chronicle* newspaper, because at that time I wanted to be a journalist. Just as I was about to leave home the bombs started; my mum pushed me down in the hall and fell on top of me, because a doodlebug had cut out over our heads and that was the danger sign. For a few minutes we thought it was going to fall on our house. It didn't – it fell a bit further on, on the Downs, about half a mile away. The house shook and we thought that the roof had fallen in – it was one of those steep, Dutch-style tiled roofs with tiles down to the first floor. My bedroom faced the direction where the bomb had dropped and as soon as we could, we dashed upstairs to see if the wall had fallen in. But it hadn't – we just lost a few tiles. So we were lucky, but it was very frightening. And that was my journalistic career over before it had started.

Margaret's mother suffered more than most:

My mother was, from a child, terrified of bangs, so you can imagine what she was like at the start of the Blitz. We sent her to stay with my uncle: he had had to leave his house at Leigh-on-Sea because it was on the front and the army wanted it, and he'd bought a cottage in Buckinghamshire and my mother went to stay with him.

One night after she'd gone, my father and I thought we heard a knock on the door. We went to look and there in the front garden was an incendiary bomb blazing away merrily – that was what we had heard as it landed. Fortunately, we all had stirrup pumps, they'd been delivered to houses, so we were able to put it out.

My father died in 1942, and it wasn't long after that that the doodlebugs started. They made an awful noise and wherever you were, you threw yourself on the ground when the noise stopped. It was surface blast from the doodlebugs – they didn't penetrate into the ground – so you weren't exactly blown up but you wanted to be as close as possible to the ground. I remember my mother getting quite hysterical and I had to slap her face to get her to stop. Obviously, the bombing was bad for everyone, but it was intolerable for her.

Along with thousands of others, David and his family took shelter in Chislehurst Caves in Kent:

The bombs came over very frequently for the first few days, until the RAF and the gun emplacements got themselves sorted out to combat them. It was very tough. We kids were playing outside, in some wooden bunks that had been removed from the caves, because the Americans had sent over some better-quality iron ones to replace them. So the wooden ones were lying about outside, waiting for someone to take them away. They were on their sides, so they formed a sort of hollow, and we were down playing in these things, hiding or jumping around, and we couldn't get out very quickly.

I saw one of these bombs cut out and start to dive. Everybody ran for the shelter, including the RAF men who were working there. We'd been brought up to think our servicemen were so brave, but even the NCO [non-commissioned officer] in charge went as white as a sheet and ran for the shelter of the caves. There was only one man who stayed behind to help us out of the bunks. Before I got to the shelter the flying bomb had landed, luckily on the other side of a huge railway embankment. The explosion was enormous and the wooden huts outside the caves seemed to lift three inches off the ground and come down again, spraying dust everywhere. Fortunately, no one was killed by that particular bomb, although there were other occasions when not everyone was so lucky.

This new wave of bombing, mostly over London and the South East, brought with it a new wave of evacuation. Having been taken to Devon by his parents earlier in the war, David was now involved in the official operation:

The penny suddenly dropped that it wasn't so safe in Kent. So we were sent to Nottingham. We spent about a week in a church hall with lots of other evacuees, without much privacy for toilets and so on. It wasn't pleasant. The man in charge knew that was so, and went to a lot of trouble to take my mother and her three children round to various very well-heeled houses where, by law, they were supposed to take you in. But every one of them had an excuse: 'We've got sickness in the house' or whatever it was. In the end he was decent enough to take my mother and sister into his house; my brother and I went to separate houses and, as it was still holiday time, we had a great time. We cycled to various RAF stations and watched planes taking off, which of course was a reminder of the war.

Then we were found an old cottage, at least eighteenth century, perhaps older, in a village called Wilford and we all moved in together again. Just behind the cottage were several great slabs of stone that served as a sort of larder, keeping food cooler and fresher than it would have been in the kitchen. Archaeologists discovered much later that those cottages had been built on the site of a medieval abbey, so the stones we made such good use of were part of the ruins.

There was a wall behind the house with big stucco tiles on top of it, but it wasn't very high and we were able to climb over into the field and play rounders and walk through the farm next door and generally have a lovely time. Nottingham had been bombed in 1941, but when we were there, there were no signs at all of the war in terms of explosions.

Sue had spent the first years of the war in rural Sussex, largely unaffected by what was going on elsewhere, but the arrival of the flying bombs changed that:

They evacuated the village, because it was in line for the V1s and V2s that were falling out of the sky. Groombridge is in a valley and on the far side of the valley, away from our little farmhouse, they had gun emplacements all the way along and told everyone to move out.

So we went to stay with a great-uncle – Uncle Dick – in Crowthorne in Berkshire. Crowthorne was (and still is) very army – it's near Camberley and Aldershot; Uncle Dick was a brigadier, I think, and a widower with a housekeeper looking after him, but he was very tolerant of having these three naughty little girls to stay with him. I remember the journey there – by train, looking at the window at the barrage balloons, which we hadn't had at Groombridge. We stayed for about two months and I don't remember much about it, but I do remember the smell of pine trees, which I hadn't known before. To this day, if I go into a pine wood, it brings me back to that place.

Before we went to Crowthorne, my mother had just planted all the vegetables in the garden she had been preparing. When it was time for us to go home she went back to Groombridge for the day, just to make sure everything was all right before she fetched us girls. She checked on the garden; everything had grown beautifully and she was very proud of it and of course those vegetables were going to help feed us through the winter. She went back to Crowthorne to fetch us and brought us home the very next day, only to find that the cows had broken in and trampled over and eaten absolutely everything.

Ten-year-old Brenda in Swanley, Kent, was also sent away from home in 1944:

After the doodlebugs started I was evacuated to a village in Devon whose name I simply can't remember. I think the school must have organised it – there was certainly a teacher on the train with us up to London and then down to Devon – but I remember that it was my choice to go. By this time I had a baby brother and sister, twins, who were nine years younger than me, so I may have wanted to get away from them, and anyway, when you're ten it's exciting to be going away from home.

Even though I don't remember the name of the village, I can see the row of four houses where I stayed. Two roads came down in a V shape, one from the station and one from wherever it was, and they joined together where these houses were; then a single road ran down to the rest of the village, the school and the posh house. I stayed in one of these houses with a girl called Margaret Dean, who lived about four houses up from us in Swanley and was two or three years younger than me. We stayed with an old lady – she must have been seventy or eighty and was very hunched. She wasn't unkind to us, but she didn't really want children to look after: she wanted someone to look after her. So I had to look after Margaret – bath her and do the washing and so on. It was quite a chore for a ten-year-old, but I was used to doing that sort of thing for the twins at home and Margaret was easier to look after than two babies.

After I'd been there a few weeks, Mum and Dad came down for a fortnight – they must have left the twins with my aunt or something – and went back without me. By that time I was homesick, so Mum came back soon afterwards to collect me. I'd loved it to start with – there were never any air-raid warnings, it was just quiet – but after a while I wanted to go back to Mum and Dad. I'm ashamed to say I don't remember what happened to Margaret Dean. I wasn't caring, I just wanted to go home. So that was my entire experience of being an evacuee. I don't think I was there for more than about six weeks.

Brian lived in Harrow and when the flying bombs came along he was sent with his brother to Aylesbury, Buckinghamshire, to stay with their grandmother and an elderly spinster aunt:

I was about seven. We were there for perhaps a year and I always remember one time when a bomber came over, my aunt told me to get under the sheets. I don't know how much protection she thought that would give me, but I did as I was told and the bomber passed over us, so perhaps she knew what she was talking about!

My grandmother and aunt spoiled us thoroughly. My mother wasn't a particularly motherly person nor a very good cook, but Gran was a farmer's daughter and had worked as a cook in a big house. When after a year our mother came to collect us she hardly recognised us because we'd put on so much weight. We'd been very happy with Gran and my aunt and were quite sorry to have to go back to Harrow.

Joan's family was lucky in being able to get to London to see their relatives there, and in having them pay return visits to Northamptonshire:

Every year we all trooped back into Tottenham, to Granny's house, but one year I think Dad must have been exhausted with the hours he was doing and he decided it would be better if we all stayed in Northamptonshire. My mum was so miserable – she was one of thirteen and she missed the family – and she informed us that no matter what Adolf Hitler did, she would be back in London next year.

My granny was a little dot. All the boys and girls in the family were six-footers, but both she and Granddad were about five foot two. Towards the end of the war, when they started dropping landmines, she always went out, just before nine o'clock, across the street to where one of her sons lived, and she'd have a glass of Guinness and listen to the nine o'clock news on the wireless. One particular night they dropped a landmine very close by and the blast carried her straight across the road – she hit their door and finished up halfway up their stairs. Two days later, the family put her on a train to Northampton, to come and stay with us. Five days after that, she said to my father, 'Will you take me down to the station and tell them I'm coming home? That bugger Adolf Hitler's not keeping me out of my house.' It was typical of the attitude of people then.

While others were being evacuated, Brian, back in Surrey after two years in Cornwall, recalls the summer of 1944 as a glorious time:

I didn't care about the bombs. I was just glad to be home again and reunited with my childhood pals…

Summer was the golden time. Released from school in mid-afternoon, my friends and I would head for Nonsuch, the park that stood at the end of the road. This had once been the site of a great palace built by Henry VIII and subsequently demolished to pay off the gambling debts of the Countess of Castlemaine, into whose hands it had passed the following century. But of course we knew nothing of this. Instead, Nonsuch was the perfect adventure playground, where I swung like Tarzan through the trees, made Robin Hood bows from young ash staves and built Apache dens among the cow parsley. Enclosed by fleets of blowsy elms, its unshorn meadows were our prairies, its hawthorn hedgerows our African savannas. In one field a landmine had fallen, blowing a deep crater in the clay that quickly filled with rain; and nature, always swift to exploit a niche, soon transformed it into a wildlife haven.

In my absence, time had healed the scars of war. Weeds and garden flowers ran riot amid the rubble, transforming bombsites into rampant jungles of raspberry canes and dense thickets of willowherb in which, sometimes, as in the ruins of a lost city, I would stumble across a back-garden statue or a marble sundial half-choked in hogweed. And over all, like a cheap perfume, hung the cloying scent of mauve-flowering buddleia bushes.

It was the summer of the great invasion; not by Rommel's Panzers but by swarms of butterflies. In the park, where trenches had been dug across the open fields to prevent German warplanes landing, thousands of tortoiseshells now sunned themselves on the tall thistles that had sprung unbidden from the disturbed clay.

As the summer advanced, clouds of migrant butterflies – peacocks, painted ladies, red admirals and clouded yellows – poured across the Channel to settle on the bombsite buddleias, where they clung in clusters, drinking in the nectar with watch-spring tongues until they were too drunk to fly.

Today the suburbia I knew – bombsites, air-raid shelters, elm trees and all – has become part of a sepia world as remote to me as Tudor England. But whenever I return to my Surrey roots, scarcely recognisable with their carports and loft conversions, my mind runs back to that butterfly year when the sun shone and the buddleia flowered and summer seemed as if it could never end.

Butterflies and doodlebugs may have been invading Britain, but the war on the Continent was taking a different turn. Despite suffering horrendous losses themselves, the Russians had won the Battle of Stalingrad in early 1943, destroying the German 6th Army and recovering much of the territory that Germany had gained over the previous two years. Italy had surrendered in September 1943; the following August, Paris was liberated. In Europe, it looked as if the end was in sight.

It didn't mean the end of casualties, though. The Allied attempt to secure the bridge at Arnhem in the Netherlands in September 1944 (filmed some thirty years later as the epic *A Bridge Too Far,* starring Sean Connery and Michael Caine) caused heavy British losses. John, at school in Yorkshire, recalls a tragedy that touched him deeply:

Early in the war the call-up of boys still at school seemed to happen frequently. We would cheer them off from the terrace at the front of the school and cheer them again if they came back in uniform. The names of those killed in action were announced in morning assembly and two had a chilling effect on us because they had been so recently one of us. A J Millichip, shot down in the RAF, had been Monitor in charge of the senior dormitory I moved to and regularly led discussions or arguments on the war before lights out. But the loss of H E Pearson at Arnhem stirred everyone. He had been a school hero, captain of the Rugby XV and the Cricket XI, and we never lost when he played (or so it was said). Head Boy, physically and academically outstanding, quickly commissioned, he was destined for much more than death among his fellow paras in a military gamble which failed.

CHAPTER 10

'IT FELT LIKE A CORK COMING OUT OF A BOTTLE'

Just as, in summer 1939, war had been seen as inevitable, so in the spring of 1945, it seemed only a matter of time before the Allies could claim victory.

John in Weymouth recalls an incident that gave a clue as to the way things were going:

On our way yet again to play summer games in the grounds of Sandsfoot Castle we walked a few hundred yards alongside the railway, and on a couple of occasions were passed by long, slow-moving trains crawling from Portland towards Weymouth. They were packed with German prisoners. We were surprised that they looked just like our boys, but sadder.

Troops returning home victorious weren't necessarily ready to celebrate. Billy remembers:

> With the end of the war in sight Bathgate collected one evening in the Steelyard to welcome home our Territorial Army contingent. Major Tom Wolfe – owner of the Steel Rolling Mill and Shovel Works – was poised on a makeshift podium in front of the Post Office. He drew breath to welcome the approaching troops, and that's as far as he got. A few words got lost in the rush towards loved ones not seen for years and the mêlée of shouting and embracing reunions. The men were in no mood for a welcome-home speech. All they wanted was – *to go home*!

Hitler's suicide on 30 April confirmed that it was all over bar the signing of documents. His successor, Grand Admiral Karl Dönitz, promptly entered into negotiations to put an end to the war and, on 7 May, the Supreme Allied Commander (and future US President) General Dwight D Eisenhower accepted Germany's unconditional surrender. The news was made public on BBC Radio late the same day, when Churchill addressed the nation:

> Hostilities will end officially at one minute after midnight tonight, Tuesday the eighth of May. We may allow ourselves a brief period of rejoicing. Today is Victory in Europe Day. Tomorrow will also be Victory in Europe Day.

But, he warned, toils and effort lay ahead. The Japanese remained unsubdued:

> We must now devote all our strength and resources to the completion of our task, both at home and abroad. Advance, Britannia. Long live the cause of freedom. God save the King.

It's unlikely many people, except those with loved ones in eastern Asia, took much notice of Churchill's warning about the Japanese. They were too busy cheering. Ros can still visualise the moment:

> I was performing in a concert, a sort of music hall in the village hall. When the news came on the radio I was actually on stage singing 'My Old Man Said Follow the Van' (I'd given up on *Cavalleria rusticana* and ballet by this time). We knew the announcement was coming, we'd been waiting all day for it, which is why we had the radio on in the background. When it came, a great cheer went up. I must have raised my arms in celebration, because I can still see the pink feather boa I was wearing slipping down on to the floor round my feet.

Bridget remembers being taken into Central London the next day:

> I think Daddy was hoping to get into the service at St Paul's, but that was jammed. So we stood outside

the Mansion House. There were masses of people and perhaps the service from St Paul's was broadcast, because we were all singing 'All People That on Earth Do Dwell'. There was a man from Holland standing next to us and he was crying. My father spoke Dutch, so they got talking and the man told him he didn't know if his family was still alive.

I was still quite little, so we came home early and didn't go in for the drunken revelry in the Mall, but I think we had fireworks in the garden – perhaps not that night but soon after, and that was something we hadn't been allowed during the war.

Miss F E Tate, living in the Fulham area of London, did stay for the evening and wrote this breathless account to her mother:

...I was going to write to you today anyhow to tell you & Dad about our excursion last night. It was simply marvellous, I've never had such a time! I had an awful cold (it's so bad today that I'm staying away from school!) & really didn't feel like going, but thought I simply must for such an occasion & because Norah wd. never have gone by herself – & now I wouldn't have missed it for anything.

We got transport to Hyde Park Corner & walked to Buckingham Palace. We just pushed our way through the crowd till we got a good place! It was huge, all over everywhere, a v. patient & good-humoured crowd.

Occasionally someone raised the chant of: 'We want the King!' in which we joined lustily – we waited like this about 20 mins. perhaps, quite prepared to wait for hours; we didn't really think we wd. see anything because other people were so much taller, & there were some in front lifting children up, & added to all this we were in our flattest of flat heels in preparation for walking home. It wasn't quite dark yet, but at last a light went up in a room behind the balcony & everyone shouted; nothing happened; then the flood lights went on, & it was the most *lovely* sight, the huge white palace against the dark blue sky, & the Royal Standard (lovely colours) lit up above it – a tremendous burst of cheering, of course, when this happened, and then out they came on the balcony & I just wish Hitler had heard the cheering – the King in naval uniform & the Queen in white evening dress with a tiara, the two princesses in blue or grey – they stood waving for several minutes & we sang 'For they are jolly good fellows'. (Norah had said we were the victims of our education & couldn't possibly enter into the spirit of the proceedings, but we are forced to the conclusion that we're not so educated as we feared!) We saw it all perfectly even if we did have to stand on tiptoe.

Finally when they went in the crowd broke up, & we decided to go to Westminster & see the floodlighting – we took our time, as every step further from the palace we had to keep looking back to see how it looked from the new angle, & even dilly-dallied to admire the chestnut

trees silhouetted in front of it. We went down Birdcage
Walk, with a horde of people, a few cars were struggling
through & most of them had self-invited passengers on
the roof. A party of service-men joined hands round a
policeman & we left them mobbing him. We cd. see
Nelson lit up in Traf. Square, & hundreds of buildings all
round – one of the best things was to see the flag floodlit
by itself here & there on top of various high places, so that
it seemed to be shining & flying unsupported in the sky –
It was a marvellous warm night and just the right amount
of wind to make the flags look perfect.

When we came into Parliament Square, still gaping
foolishly at everything & not hurrying at all, we heard
terrific cheering in front of us – we ran like mad to see
what was happening & arrived *just* as the Prime Minister
had appeared on a balcony! It couldn't have been better
timed if it had been a Cook's tour. We saw him perfectly
– It was the big building on the corner, I think it's
the Min. of Health but I'm not sure – it was floodlit
& flying the biggest & best flags, scores of them, the
RAF flag conspicuous, from where we were standing.
Everyone shouted, of course, & at last Mr Churchill
made a speech, which I'm sure was impromptu – I wish
I could remember it all; if it appears in the *D. Telegraph*
or any other paper you lay hands on, do please cut it out
for me? He was thanking London for their courage, but
nobody wanted to be serious & he knew just the right
jokes to make. He began: 'My dear friends – (the first
of continual interruptions, everyone had to cheer at this

& at everything) 'I hope you have had two happy days'
(loud applause). He then said not to forget that victory
and rejoicing were very hard won; 'You have been
attacked by a terrible & implacable foe –' (everyone said
'ooo!' in dismal tones). 'I am now addressing myself to
the Cockneys – and any Britishers who may be among
us tonight' (roars of laughter). He said that the civilians
had backed up the fighting Services nobly – 'our Army
& our Air Force – & let us not forget our glorious
Navy' – which brought forth cheers, of course – 'We
didn't have to surrender because London squealed she
was getting hurt;' ('no bloody fear') 'You stood like a
hippopotamus – no, like a rhinoceros! – and showed the
world you could take it – I knew London would never
give in!' (Frantic applause.) 'Long may you be the heart
of a free & decent world.'

Then, after Churchill had led a rousing chorus or two of
'Rule Britannia':

He had terrific applause, doubled when he waved his hat
& puffed his cigar – which he did deliberately at well-
chosen moments throughout his speech. After he went
in, we decided to go onto Westminster Bridge to get a
view of the lighting all along the river – other people had
some similar idea. There was such a noise going on that
we never even heard Big Ben strike eleven, tho' we were
on the bridge at the time.

People had gone quite mad & were linking arms &

sweeping up & down the road, or joining on behind each other & trotting about in long files like children playing. We wandered about in a daze saying, 'How marvellous – look! how marvellous!' just as we did over the apple-blossom at Kew, until Norah said, 'This is better than Kew, let's never go home.'

Around the country, the celebrations were a strange mixture of the joyful and the subdued. Charlotte was at school in Speyside when the news came through:

We had a special service – we learned 'Jerusalem', which we hadn't sung before. We had two days' holiday and all sorts of unusual things were arranged. We had picnics, lovely picnics – we must have had gorgeous weather, which you don't necessarily expect in Scotland, but we did. And I remember telling myself seriously, 'This means people will stop being killed.' I wasn't very specific, but looking back on it that is quite a grown-up thought. I'd been aware of loss, though. I can remember one of my parents' great friends being killed and the news coming through to them. They were pretty quiet about it, but I can remember the feeling of distress.

Maggie in Barry remembers:

… a lot of cheering and shouting and people letting bangers off. This was most unusual, so I asked my mother what was going on.

'It means the war is over,' she explained. 'There's not going to be any more bombing.'

But I don't think I really took it in. I'd never known a life without sirens and bombing – I don't know how it was for the adults, but for me it was the norm.

Billy's memories also include mixed emotions...

When war in Europe ended, it was announced in school in the middle of the morning – in the middle of a music lesson – and we were told we could have the rest of the day off. The initial reaction was muted. Maybe because it had been expected and when we walked home from school things seemed no different from when we had come to school earlier in the day.

With the cessation of hostilities, bonfires to celebrate were the order of the day. I see myself approaching The Elms – Major Wolfe's house at the top of our road. Am I on my way to ask permission to have a bonfire there or to ask for help from the factory with it? I know not, but my mother did later remind me that I was the instigator of the building of the bonfire opposite the Wee Mair school. I recall going round the houses collecting the bric-a-brac of six years of austerity that could now be discarded – a bamboo curtain rail sticks in my mind, and a small barrel of tar from Wolfe's, which was set right in the middle of the heap. Its melted unconsumed contents pavemented the site of the bonfire for at least twenty years thereafter.

As do Connie's:

My sister was married on 5 May 1945, the Saturday before VE Day. It may not have been announced formally, but we knew that the war was won. I remember we went to the Pier Head after the wedding and all the lights were on. It was such fun, after the darkness that we'd got used to. They went to London for their honeymoon and stood outside Buckingham Palace, waving at the Royal Family. But what I remember most clearly is that it had been my birthday in April. My mother had managed to gather together the ingredients to make a cake and had decorated it with 'Happy Birthday' and everything – then she realised that Blanche would need a wedding cake. So the 'Happy Birthday' was scraped off and the cake was saved for the wedding day. Given that this was not long after my disappointment over the dance dress [see page 99/100], I was very fed up.

The *Luton News* cheerfully reported that 'within a few hours streets and roads were transformed as if by miracle. The drab, grey streets of wartime became peacetime avenues of red, white and blue in profuse array.' Pauline remembers it well:

My mother took my brother and myself to New Bedford Road, where everyone was celebrating: dancing and singing and laughing. We three were pulled into a circle and joined hands and danced. All singing and all dancing, we gravitated down the road towards our lovely park in Luton, Wardown, where we were still singing and dancing on the grass around the bandstand.

Communal celebrations were the order of the day, as Tony recalls:

Everybody got together and arranged street parties. The mums made jam tarts and a few extra things like that. You might be able to scratch up a bit of a jelly, but basically it was cakes and little sandwiches. People brought out chairs and tables – picnic tables or card tables with green baize tops. There were different parties going on on different days, so if you were friendly with someone in the next street you could join their party or they could come round to yours.

Audrey in Weymouth remembers similar parties:

At the end of the war we had a street party for VE Day – the weather wasn't very good, and we didn't have very much but lots of trestle tables came out, I guess from the church hall, and everybody must have provided sandwiches – paste sandwiches – and some sort of cake. I used to have a photo and I'm sure we were wearing fancy hats. All the children were seated at the tables and all the adults were standing about drinking tea.

...as does Margaret in Walthamstow:

On VE Day we went down to the bombsite at the bottom of our road and from somewhere – they must have been pre-war – somebody had got some fireworks. They hadn't been allowed, obviously, during the war, so we had fireworks and it was pretty amazing. I think we sang – but anyway, it was a wonderful feeling, I must say, a wonderful feeling of relief.

Relief was uppermost in Nancy's mind, too:

We had all sorts of little treats. People dug out things and made a cake out of something – you get very inventive when you're short of things. But everybody was very happy. It was so lovely to think that it was over – it felt like a cork coming out of a bottle. I think the blackout was the worst. It was awful being in the dark all the time.

June in Andover wasn't able to join the celebrations on the day:

I was at work on VE Day. I was not quite fifteen and I had a job at the local police station because they were terribly short of people to work there. There were two of us on the telephones; we did turn and turn about, taking messages as they came from headquarters at Winchester. Not only on VE Day but for several days before messages had been coming in at a tremendous rate. There were a lot of defence regulations at that time and some of them were taken off very quickly, so that people could more or less go out and do what they liked. For example, there had been a regulation forbidding anyone from ringing bells, including for a while church bells, without permission and that went – we were allowed to ring the bells on our bicycles or any other bells we had.

Another one was rattles, the kind you have at football matches; they had been banned from football, because they were to be used to give warning of a gas attack. So suddenly you were allowed to rattle your rattle at football again, or anywhere else. All the noise regulations came off immediately, so we could all go out and make as much noise as we liked. And you could tear down the blackout curtains and have as much light as you liked – you didn't have to have tape across your torch to guard it. There were all sorts of little things that we'd got used to doing that we didn't have to do any more.

I couldn't go out and celebrate, because we weren't given the time off. All the police were brought in on duty. I'd done the early shift that day, but I was still in the station in the afternoon and I was allowed to go upstairs to a room they had and listen to Churchill's speech on the radio. Then I think we all made tea, and the people in uniform went off to parade round the town and make sure reasonable order was kept.

A few days later we had a proper celebration, with a bonfire out of town somewhere, and people were arranging teas outside. They were especially for the children, but I think everyone more or less joined in and contributed what they could. Fruit jellies were quite the thing. Gelatine was off-ration, and lots of people grew raspberries or strawberries, so you got what fruit you could and crushed it and made jelly. Of course no one had a fridge, so you kept it in the coolest place around – probably on the floor of the larder.

Relieved or not, some people were just too tired to enjoy themselves. Like many people, Shirley's parents had done war work as well as their day jobs:

My mother was an ARP warden and my father a sergeant in the Home Guard, so they were doing this at night and their normal work during the day. Years later, I asked my mother what she and my father had done on the day war ended and she said, 'We didn't do anything. It was summer and we sat on either side of the fireplace, looking at each other and we never said a word. For the first time in years, we were allowed to feel tired.'

I understand about being allowed to feel tired, but what really impressed me during the war – and this was one of the things that was so character-forming – was that everybody swung into a besieged island mentality so quickly. The war taught you very quickly to prioritise, not to make a fuss, make do and mend, and survive on the minimum. There was a strong feeling of 'Britons never, never shall be slaves', a grim determination to do whatever was necessary to keep the Germans out. The spirit of the country – we were united in our attitude. My parents were bombed out three times, and I remember – again, years later – my mother heard me telling someone this and afterwards she said to me, 'No, we were not bombed out.'

I said, 'Mum! Three times! Windows out, doors down, roof off...'

And she said, 'Yes, we were bombed. We were never *bombed out*.'

That really illustrates the feeling.

John, now aged eleven, went home to London after five years away:

I remember hearing on the radio that the war was over. That would have been in May. And in the September I know I was back in London, attending the local grammar school. But I don't remember anything in between. It's funny, because I recall vividly being evacuated – I can see my five-year-old self on the platform at Paddington Station, stepping onto the train, with a little knapsack on my back with my name on it, and saying goodbye to my mother – but I don't remember anything about going home at the end of the war. I suppose my parents came to collect me, but I just don't know. And of course I had no friends in London, so until I got to school and made new friends, I didn't go out to play. It was a whole different world.

Ros remembers one special celebration:

Not long after VE Day, I went with my parents to a dinner at the Royal Naval and Military Club in Piccadilly, which had been the headquarters for General de Gaulle and the Free French. It must have been in honour of General de Gaulle – he was certainly there. Goodness knows why we were invited: my father was something senior at the Ministry of Food, but only in our local area – he wasn't as senior as all that. Anyway, there we were and at one point somebody wanted to attract de Gaulle's attention, so they threw an olive pit at him and it landed on our table instead of his. There must have been speeches and probably something more exciting to eat than we had been used to during the war, but all I remember is this little olive pit rolling around on the white tablecloth.

Those who were expecting life to get back to normal straight away were to be disappointed. Sam remembers his first seaside holiday:

At the very end of the war – the summer of 1945, when I was not quite seven and my sister not quite five – we went on the first holiday that I can remember. We went to the seaside in Essex, to Walton-on-the-Naze. When we got to the beach, what my sister and I wanted was sand and castles and spades and buckets. And sea, after all. We may never have been to the seaside before, but I at least had read *Rupert Bear* annuals and Enid Blyton and I knew what the seaside *should* be like. I'd had both measles and mumps by this time, so I had spent quite a lot of time in bed and got well acquainted with Rupert Bear. Another odd thing I remember is that what they gave me to eat while I was recovering, for reasons unknown to me, were gooseberry-jam sandwiches, which I've never been able to stomach since.

Anyway, to get back to Walton-on-the-Naze, to reach the sea you had to go down a carefully delineated path, beside which on both sides were coiled barbed wire and large signs saying, 'Beware mines'. So you actually had to walk through a partial minefield to get to the beach – which had metal crosses all over it to defend it. The Essex coast had been one of the possibilities for Operation Sea Lion – Hitler's planned invasion of Britain; he would certainly have considered it as a possible route to London. And our beach still showed the evidence of that.

Margaret in Walthamstow has a similar memory:

In July or August 1945, I developed a bad chest infection; I was due to be married in the September and I was told I ought to go to the seaside to help me recover. My mother had a friend who lived in Herne Bay, so I went to stay with her and I remember walking along the beach, which had very recently been cleared of mines. I was petrified, quite honestly, that any moment I was going to step on one. And there was still lots of barbed wire around.

Nor did victory bring an immediate return to prosperity. Maggie and her mother moved back from Barry to Folkestone:

In the summer of 1945, Father came home with his demob suit – a grey pinstripe, with a pair of shoes, a shirt and a tie – and a grey blanket, and that was all. Down at the bottom of Remembrance Hill there was a great big warehouse where they handed out the clothes to people being demobbed.

Father had a new job in Folkestone and Mother was planning to reopen the boarding house she had run before the war, but when we came home we discovered that a buzz bomb had come down on it. We lost every single bit of furniture. Not only that, there was a hole in the top of the house. Goodness knows how long it had been like that. All the ceilings were in ruins; all the windows were shattered and all the glass had been blown into the walls. So three of us pulled every piece of glass out of the walls; Mother put sheets over the ceilings to stop the plaster falling on guests; got the windows mended and started up again. A lot of people who'd come before the war – the holidaymakers – heard that she had opened up again and they started coming back. She'd got a lot of second-hand furniture from a local place called Walter's with the promise that she'd be able to pay for it in six months or a year, and she did. Then when she could afford it, she went back to Mr Walter, who'd been so decent to her, and bought all her new stuff from him. My mother really was a worker – she just rolled her sleeves up and got on with things.

One almost immediate result of the peace was the need to address what was happening in Parliament. The coalition government had been a temporary measure, intended only to see the country through the war; Churchill now suggested that it remain in place until victory over Japan was assured. But the Labour Party refused to cooperate and, only weeks after VE Day, Churchill resigned and was appointed head of a caretaker government until an election could be held. Scheduled for 5 July 1945, it would be the first general election for ten years.

John was by this time sixteen and still at school:

We boys had followed the war avidly, battle by battle, front by front; and, I suppose, we were indeed quite knowledgeable. In the way that nowadays a schoolboy might be able to explain to you why Tottenham Hotspur was having a losing streak, we were well informed about El Alamein. (In 1940, aged eleven, I remember precociously asking my mother on the train back to school how I would get home at Christmas if, like France, we were invaded and partitioned. She said, 'I'm sure we shall find a way.')

Towards the end of the war, when the creation of the United Nations was being mooted, we started to look towards the future. The Conservative Party, with the possible exception of Rab Butler, who was only in his early forties, seemed like the party of the past. I don't remember being aware of Clement Attlee, the leader of the Labour Party, who of course became Prime Minister. Herbert Morrison and Ernest Bevin were more in the public eye.

When the general election campaign began we sixth formers were encouraged to visit local hustings meetings, with attendant masters. The meetings were usually held in state school class-rooms. Arthur Greenwood, who had been a Labour member of Churchill's wartime cabinet, was seeking re-election in Wakefield and we were keen to see the great man, but we had to leave before he arrived. (I can still remember the grim Catholic primary school-room, painted dark green and without windows. Its only decoration was the text 'Thou God see-est me', a threat more than an encouragement.)

Remember, there hadn't been an election for ten years, so to sixteen-year-old schoolboys it was a new experience. Going to hustings with one of our masters, who was interested in politics and later became an MP, was quite instructive.

Churchill's Conservative colleagues expected a landslide victory for 'the man who had won the war'. On 5 July, the country showed that it had other ideas. The voters did indeed produce a landslide, but not in Churchill's favour. A 10 per cent swing to Labour gave that party its first ever overall majority and installed the unassuming Clement Attlee in Downing Street.

Martin, aged twenty-two and in the RAF, remembers the result as a great shock:

Many thought that it was a betrayal of Winnie, who was widely considered to have been the person who pulled the nation together at its lowest hour.

Perhaps, because he was such a great wartime leader and fighting in the west had finally come to an end, memories of his past record of his use of troops to put down peacetime internal disputes went against him. Of course VE Day ended the fear of more loss of life at home, but rationing was still with us and those discharged from the services would have had more faith in Labour to provide and preserve employment for the many. At the time trade unions had a large say in Labour Party policy and were responsible for a large portion of the Labour vote.

Whatever the reason, it did seem like a betrayal of, in some people's view, the Saviour of our Nation.

Nancy, too, recalls a feeling of shock:

At least it was to me – I don't suppose it was to everybody. But there was a different mood in the country. My husband was in the Eighth Army and he'd fought in the desert, in North Africa; he detested Churchill. He said he was an autocrat and an aristocrat who didn't think about people, he just thought about numbers, and he sacrificed soldiers. I'd always thought Churchill was good, but my husband made me see another side to him. He was necessary at the time – his determination and his ruthlessness were what was needed – but perhaps it was time for a change.

On the other hand, June in Andover remembers the result as a cause for celebration:

The Labour Party had been working in the factories and all over the place and I don't think the Conservatives realised how eager people were for a change and a new start. Before the war, of course, unemployment had been very bad and unemployment pay wasn't at all good; Labour was promising lots of reforms – including the National Health Service, which they introduced. We were part of Basingstoke constituency at that time and we did return the Conservative candidate; the Labour candidate was a lady and perhaps that put some people off – it was a long time before they started really putting females into Parliament.

Joan in Peterborough came from a Labour-supporting family:

My father was a railwayman and a union man, and he was delighted with the election result – he'd been describing Churchill as a warmonger well before the Second World War; I don't think he'd forgiven him for the first one. As a loyal Labour man, he didn't like anyone who changed political parties, whichever way they went. And Churchill had done that not once but twice in the course of his career.

The other thing that was good, as far as I was concerned, was that the post-war Labour government introduced the Welfare State and particularly the National Health Service. Before that, you had to pay the doctor in the same way you paid the grocer or anybody else. During the war I had two children under the age of five and at one point my son was ill enough to need the doctor out. I'd been saving up for net curtains and I had to spend those carefully squirrelled-away shillings to pay for the doctor's visit. So the introduction of the NHS seemed almost like a reward for what we ordinary people had done and put up with during the war.

While those in Britain were either reeling from shock or looking forward to forging a new way of life, the Allied forces finally forced Japan to surrender in September 1945, four months after war had ended in Europe. Mervyn remembers celebrating 'Victory over Japan' in August:

By the last summer of the war I was a student in Cheltenham. We celebrated VE Day by having a free day. Victory over Japan came in the summer holidays and I remember a bonfire and bun fight on Nibley Knoll, a local beauty spot: the monument there was visible from our kitchen window and to this day gives panoramic views over the lower Severn Valley. I'm sure everyone was in a festive mood that night, though food would have been in short supply – probably just something like sandwiches and maybe a plain cake. We may have won the war but we hadn't won the peace. Food rationing was still severe; in fact, it was only after the war that bread became rationed: the country couldn't afford to buy the wheat.

At the event was a troop of Girl Guides from Bristol, with whom we lads had platonic chats. Strangely enough, many years later I was at a dog show and the conversation turned to events at the end of the war. One of the group mentioned that she had been in Guide camp at Nibley and had spent the evening at the monument. Small world indeed.

Sylvia, too, remembers VJ Day (Victory Over Japan) as being special:

I remember the general excitement of VE Day. It was such a thrill and such a relief to think that it was over. But VJ Day was actually my sister's wedding day. It been arranged before they knew that was going to happen and everything was chaotic. My father had leave to come and give my sister away. Our family had moved around so much that we didn't really have anywhere we called home, so the wedding took place near Norwood Junction, where the groom's parents lived. They'd booked a local place for the reception and then it was announced that the day they'd chosen was going to be celebrated as VJ Day. Pubs were going to be open all day, which was unusual then, and in all the upheaval the hotel forgot the reception.

London seemed so full. I had to go through it to get from Luton to Croydon by train and there were crowds everywhere. Just so many people. Everybody was laughing, dancing – the excitement was quite something. There had been excitement for VE Day, but this was all that and more.

But of course what had brought the war in the East to an end was the dropping of atomic bombs on the Japanese cities of Hiroshima and Nagasaki on 6 and 9 August. Norm's ship, HMS *Anson*, was in the port of Kobe at the end of that month: it had been part of the convoy that accepted the Japanese surrender of Hong Kong and was due to be part of the official surrender on 2 September. Granted shore leave before that ceremony, Norm and his friend Bill took the opportunity to visit Hiroshima:

We knew that it was only a short train ride from Kobe, but not speaking Japanese, we weren't sure how to get there. The Americans in port helped us find the station – for some reason we didn't have to pay. The ride was about twenty minutes, we knew where to alight and soon we were standing on another platform, not knowing where to go or what to do.

Again, the Yanks came to our rescue. They seemed genuinely concerned about us, and about what was happening in Hiroshima. We were taken by jeep to the outskirts of the city and told to walk with care until we saw a bridge ahead of us. Then, one of the Americans warned, we should prepare ourselves for what we were about to see.

Bill and I made our way along the rock-filled road to the remains of a sturdy bridge. Its iron girders were twisted into strange shapes, many having melted in the heat; the thick, heavy wooden supports were almost burned through. From the size of the bridge the river beneath it must have been substantial, but now there was hardly any water in it. Where had it gone, we wondered.

Then we looked beyond the bridge and gaped in horror. The once proud city of Hiroshima had been completely flattened. There was almost literally nothing but rubble. Just the wreck of a building or two. It had been a city of 350,000 people, and on that day we did not see or meet a soul. We learned subsequently that as many as 80,000 had been killed when the bomb fell and a further 80,000 later died of their injuries.

There were so many holes in the bridge that we decided the only safe way to cross it was to crawl, clinging to whatever we could find to keep our balance. On the other side, the road stretched ahead for about half a mile; over to our right, we noticed something shining brightly from the rubble. It turned out to be blocks of glass that had at one time been bottles and were now reduced to great lumps. We'd stumbled across a bottle factory – completely destroyed, like everything around it. Not knowing anything about contamination, we picked up some small samples to take back to the ship.

As we turned to go back to the bridge, we noticed the remains of what had been a brick wall and on it the shadows of four people, vaporised against the bricks. Two big, two small – Mum, Dad and two children. Many people have since asked me, 'Are you sure?' and I can only reply, 'I saw what I saw.'

Try to imagine the town or city you love completely, and I mean completely, flattened by just one bomb. Yes, it brought about the end of the war, but of all the horrors I had seen, this is the one that has remained embedded in my mind all these years. I still often wonder how anyone could have done this to their fellow human beings.

And yet, and yet… Eileen echoes the feeling of many when she says:

It may sound awful, but I felt that the war years were the best years of my life. It lasted from when I was fourteen to when I was twenty and, although we didn't use the word then, I was a proper teenager. You didn't worry about things. I worked in a factory, and the friendliness of the women and the girls was lovely. We made cases for bullets and that sort of thing – as far as I was interested, at that age, in knowing what I was doing. I was getting paid and I was with a lot of other girls my age and that was all I cared about.

People's attitude was very different from what it is

today. You'd go into work in the morning and people would say, 'Oh, lovely to see you, Eileen – were you all right last night? Wasn't it terrible?' and that sort of thing, because of course there would have been a raid. And sometimes there were people who *weren't* all right and that brought us to earth but, otherwise, it was just life.

Nancy, now one hundred and one and looking back on her early twenties, puts it this way:

If you asked me for one word to sum up how I feel now about the war, I'd have to say 'affection', because it was a lovely time, really. I was very lucky. I didn't see any bad conflict, and we only had nice times. Although there were shortages, everyone was in the same state and we made do with what we had.

The best of times, the worst of times indeed. Kate, on a Yorkshire bus just before VE Day, overheard this exchange between two old men:

'What'll ye do when t'war's over? Are ye going t' celebrate or are ye goin' t' praise God?'

'Ee, I don't know. They say ye should praise God, but then 'E's made a helluva mess of fruit trees this year.'

ACKNOWLEDGEMENTS

As I said in the acknowledgements to my *Christmas at War*, a book like this literally cannot be written without the enthusiasm and interest of a great many people. So thanks first of all to those who scoured their address books and their Facebook friends to find me willing interviewees: Ann, Cec, Gill, Julia and Peter, Kathy, Kyle, Lois, Rebecca, Rosey, Sheena, the two Sues, Susie and Tracey. Thanks also to Sheila Bellis, Mary Bradley, Debbie Chisholm, Anne Falconer, Lynn Jones, Sarah Lowry, Marilyn Neil, Hilary Oates and Paula Tyler for facilitating; Rebecca Reed for lending me the diary of her grandfather William Davis; and Joan Berry for organising such an enjoyable and productive tea party.

Even more important, though, are the contributors themselves. I am immensely grateful to all of the following, who remembered so much that had happened nearly eighty years ago and were happy to share it with me:

Brenda Alexander; Eileen Baker; the late Roy Bartlett; Jenny Bridges; the late Brenda Burrage; Joyce Cable; Martin Catty; John Chelsom; Bridget Clarke; Shirley Conran; Hazel Davey; Deidre Davies; John Davis; Joan Denton; Kathy Dunn; Sue Egerton-Jones; Sheila Evans; Jean Fogg; Albert Frears; Beryl Ginger; Sylvia Green; Ellen Grout; Charlotte Halliday; Maggie Harrison; Bob Hawkins; Irvine Hunt; Brian Jackman; the late David Johnson; Jean King; Norman Lewis, Marjorie Rogers and Stan Lewis; Billy Millan; Brenda Mole; Connie Neil; the late Mervyn Philpott; Audrey Russell; Sam Simmonds; Joan Sinclair; Dolly Sinden; Margaret Slater; Anne Smith; Jeanne and Paul Strang; John Thompson; Marjorie Thorpe; John Tiranti; Nancy Titman; Valerie Warwick; Joan White; Ros Wilden Brown and Wendy Winfield. Special thanks to Pauline and Tony who, in addition to being warm-hearted hosts and great raconteurs, allowed me to quote from the memoir of Pauline's father, Herbert Draper, and to June Harris, not only for her memories but for suggesting that the war had been the best of times and the worst of times.

The extract on page 27 is taken from an interview with Dr John Goldsmith, reference number 61982, from the collections of the Royal College of Physicians; and those on pages 22 and 139 are reproduced courtesy of Gunnersbury Park Museum. Thanks (again) to Sarah Lowry for putting me in touch with both these sources, and to Amy Dobson at Gunnersbury for her help.

I have also quoted extensively from private papers held

in the Documents and Sound Section of the Imperial War Museum and am grateful to Simon Offord and the rest of the museum staff for their efficiency and helpfulness. The extracts on pages 7, 114, 115, 175 and 272 are by James Cheeseman (Documents.15598); pages 25, 91, 209 and 238 by Rose Cottrell (Documents.13128); page 32 Gwen Green (née Clements, Documents.2545); pages 37, 109, 217 and 316 by Kathleen Margaret (Kate) Crawley (Documents.2760, used by permission of Derek and Morag Crawley); page 56 from the Balendoch Evacuation Diary (Documents. 13646); pages 90, 164 and 208 from the papers of Ernest & Evelyn Harwood (Documents.16878, by permission of Michael Harwood); page 105 J W Thraves (Documents.7776, by permission of Robert Thraves); pages 112, 132, 138 and 151 by Phyllis Warner (Documents.3208); page 134 by Frank Hurd (Documents.4833); pages 194, 197 and 252 by Barbara Fisher (Documents.3817); page 249 and 267 by Alex Savidge (Documents.921); page 254 by Jimmy Green; page 255 by L E Anderson; page 292 Miss F E Tate (Documents. 3096); page 256 by Michael Reynell (Documents.17372). Some of the background information on the Women's Land Army came from the papers of Olive Kersley (Documents.972).

The extracts from Vere Hodgson's diaries on pages 75, 113 and 153 are taken from *Few Eggs and No Oranges*, published by Persephone Books. Information about the Canadian role in the D-Day landings came from http://www.junobeach.info/

Every effort has been made to contact the copyright holders for material quoted in the book; if anyone I have not been able to find would care to get in touch via the publishers, I shall be happy to acknowledge them in future editions.

BIBLIOGRAPHY

Bartlett, Roy *A Little Boy's War* (Authorhouse, 2006)

Bougaardt, Richard *D-Day: Normandy revisited* (Chaucer Press, 2004)

Harris, June Mary *Growing Up in Wartime Andover* (Andover History and Archaeology Society, 1999)

Harrisson, Tom *Living through the Blitz* (Collins, 1976)

Hodgson, Vere *Few Eggs and No Oranges: Diaries 1940–45* (Persephone Books, 1999)

Hunt, Irvine *School House* (2017)

Mosley, Leonard *Backs to the Wall: London under fire 1940–1945* (Weidenfeld & Nicolson, 1971)

Patten, Marguerite *We'll Eat Again: a collection of recipes from the war years* (Hamlyn, 1985)

Sladen, Chris 'Holidays at Home in the Second World War' in *Journal of Contemporary History*, Vol. 37, no. 1 (January 2002), pp. 67–89 (Sage Publications)

Smitten City: the story of Portsmouth under Blitz (1945, revised 1981, Portsmouth Publishing and Printing)

Taggart, Caroline *Christmas at War: Heartwarming true stories of how Britain came together on the Home Front* (John Blake, 2018)

Dan Farnworth is an ambulance medic based in the nor' v
services for sixteen years. He is the founder of Our Blue Light, a campaign to raise awareness of mental health issues in the emergency services, and won the ITV NHS Heroes Award for Mental Health Champion of the Year.